HUMAN RIGHTS VIOLATION

HUMAN RIGHTS VIOLATION

Contemporary Concerns & Remedies

Jagmohan Mishra

FORWARD BOOKS

NEW DELHI • GUWAHATI • VISAKHAPATNAM

FORWARD BOOKS
4649-B/21, Ansari Road
Darya Ganj, New Delhi - 110 002
Ph.: 23263193 / 9811582579 / 09435116718
Fax: 011-23263193
Email: ektabooks@yahoo.com
www.akanshapublishinghouse.com

Human Rights Violation: Contemporary Concerns & Remedies

First Published 2011
ISBN 978-81-909742-1-9

[The responsibility for the facts stated, conclusions reached etc., is entirely that of the author. The publisher is not responsible for them, whatsoever.]

PRINTED IN INDIA

Published by Forward Books, New Delhi and Printed at S.N Printers, Delhi.

CONTENTS

Preface

"There is no man so good, who, were he to submit his thoughts and actions to the laws, would not deserve hanging ten times in his life."

—Michael de Montaigno

Respect for human rights of every person is an inherent trait of man. Training for this was imparted to children in every household by way of moral and ethical values. With the development of civilizatior and state authority to regulate social order, emerged the necessity of policing and judiciary. With the passes of time under contemporary circumstances the state and its law enforcing agencies became powerful and authoritarian, thus started the perpetration of inhuman treatment on the innocent people in the name of maintaining law and order. Police system gradually became brutal and corrupt.

No doubt, anti-social elements have been there from very ancient time. Delinquents and criminals, were found in every society—since corruption and crime have been part and parcel of human behaviour.

The contemporary society is infested with criminal activities of all sorts. International conflicts, war, terrorism, illegal trade activities, occupation of weaker states by the powerful and theft, robberies, murder, crime against women, smuggling and trafficking in women and children etc. are the order of day. To check these state's machinery works hard. But state agencies are more brutal than the criminals. Illegal detention, arbitrary arrests, torture and inhuman treatment of detainees, prisoners, under-trials are rampant. Custodial deaths are common. Earlier people did not have the voice against these. Now with judicial and media activism these cases frequently come to public notice.

In the present book we have made an attempt to collate vital information on human rights violation, various types of inhuman treatment like torture, custodial violence and deaths, disappearances, and police atrocities etc. The rights of victims, statutory measures available and response of civil society and other salient issues are elaborately dealt with. The text is supported by facts and figures, case studies, court judgements etc. The information is gathered under the following headings—Introduction; Torture: A Stigma on Civil Society; Patterns of Torture and Victims; Impunity: Condoning Custodial Violence; Custodial Violence: Causes and Concerns; Police Atrocities and Judicial Measures; Measures for Curbing Torture; Standards and Actions; Disappearances; Appendices; Glossary & Bibliography etc.

Hopefully, this will serve as a reference book for academics, police and law enforcing agencies, human rights activists, policy planners and administrators besides general readers concerned with cause of human rights.

We have drawn upon works of many experts in the field while collating the information. We express our gratefulness to them all. Though every care is taken to furnish accurate information, there may have crept in some inaccuracies, which we will rectify if brought to ournotice by learned readers. We are also grateful to our colleagues and friends for inspiring, guiding and assisting us in different stages of this work. Finally we are thankful to our publishers for evincing interest in this and publishing it meticulously within shortest possible time.

—Jagmohan Mishra

1

INTRODUCTION

> Anybody can become angry—that is easy; but to be angry with the right person, and to the right degree, and at the right time, and for the right purpose, and in the right way—that is not within everybody's power and is not easy.
>
> —*Aristotle*

Human rights are natural fundamental rights of every human being for protection of which international and national standards are there. The state has the obligation of protecting human rights. But it is seen in one pretext or other often human rights are violated by the State and its agencies. Detention in police custody, torture, custodial violence and deaths, disappearances are frequent and mundane occurrences in different parts of the world. In our country the police system is of worst kind and is most corrupt—hence the cases of human rights violations take place frequently. Even our security forces operating in different disturbed areas are also blamed for human rights violations.

Most of such cases do not come to public notice. But thanks to current media boom and to some extent judicial activism, now such cases cannot remain unnoticed/concealed for long.

What is Torture ?

Torture has been defined as infliction of severe physical pain upon a person in order to force him to act against his will or to punish him. As early as in 1850 the Torture Commission of India attempted to define 'torture', and quoted Dr. Johnson who said that, "torture was fair by which guilt is punished or confession extorted". The World Medical Association in (WMA) its Tokyo Declaration (1975) gave a clearly stated definition of torture. The Declaration states that 'torture is deliberate, systematic or wanton infliction of physical or mental suffering by one or more persons acting alone or on the orders of any authority, to force another person to yield information, to make a confession, or for any other reason."

Further, Chet Scrngnar defines torture as an intentional trauma deliberately conceived by vilemen to systematically cause pain and suffering to selected individuals ultimately ending with the physical and psychological collapse of the victims. The old notion was that the main purpose was to make people talk. From 1960 onwards, it should be seen that the intention of the torture was to make the general population keep silent and it is this kind of torture which tries to curb and throttle democratic systems.

Torture is rightly considered as the most heinous violation of human rights as it constitutes the very denial of the essence of human rights, namely, recognition that each living being has a personality of his own which has to be respected. Torture takes many forms and course in widely divergent situations. No country, whatever its political system or ideological colour, is indeed free from this scar.

Freedom from torture and other cruel, inhuman, degrading treatment or punishment is proclaimed as a fundamental right of human beings in the Universal Declaration of Human Rights. Article 5 of the Declaration lays down "none shall be subjected to torture or to cruel, inhuman, degrading treatment or punishment." Again Article 7 of the International Covenant on Civil and Political Rights reiterates that none shall be subjected to torture, and in particular no one shall be subjected, without his free consent, to medical or scientific experimentation." Article 4(2) of the Covenant on Civil and Political Rights clearly stipulates that freedom from torture remains a basic non-derogable human right even in times of public emergency "which threatens the life of the nation and the existence of which is officially proclaimed."

Convention Against Torture and other Cruel, Inhuman or Degrading Treatment or Punishment was adopted by the United Nations General Assembly on 10th December, 1984 (Resolution 39/46). It went into force in June, 1987 when 20 Member States ratified the Convention. By 1st of September, 1996, 99 States out of it 187 Member States of U.N. had so far ratified it. Earlier in 1975, the United Nations General Assembly had adopted unanimously a Declaration aimed at banning torture. This was mainly of moral and political value. This was followed by a legally binding text. The Convention requires State parties to take adequate and effective steps to prevent torture in any territory under their jurisdiction. Each State party shall ensure that all acts of torture become offences under its Criminal law and shall make these offences punishable by appropriate penalties which take into account their grave nature (Article 4). No exceptional circumstances, such as war or public emergency, can be invoked to justify torture (Article 2). Obedience to order from a superior authority or public servant will not be accepted as a justification for torture under any circumstance.

The Convention provides for prosecution or extradition of persons alleged to have committed acts of torture and State parties are called on to afford one another assistance in connection with judicial proceedings concerning acts of torture. The Convention calls on State parties to ensure that education and information regarding the prohibition against torture are included in the training of law-enforcement, civil, military, medical personnel and other persons involved in the custody, interrogation or treatment of detenus. Article 14 of the Convention provides that the victim of an act of torture obtains redress and has an enforceable right to fair and adequate compensation. Other forms of cruel, inhuman or degrading punishment as defined in the Convention which may be committed by persons acting in an official capacity are also prohibited.

The implementation of the Convention is monitored by the Committee against Torture consisting of 10 experts elected by the State parties to the Convention and serving in their personal capacity. State parties to the Convention are required to report regularly to the committee on the measures they have taken to give effect to the provisions of the Convention. Under Article 20 of the Convention, if the committee receives well-founded information that torture is being systematically practised, in the territory of a State party, it will ask the State party to cooperate in the examination of the information and to this end to submit observations with regard to the information concerned.

1984 Convention not only prohibits torture but also forbids inhuman action on a less macroscopic scale-cruel inhuman, degrading treatment or punishment. Thus there is "tightening of the normative mesh" with a view to reducing the scope of discretion of the States. The Committee may also make an enquiry, including a visit to the territory of the State party concerned, with its agreement. The proceedings of the committee are confidential, but the committee may decide to include a summary account of the result of the proceedings in its annual report to the State parties and to the General Assembly.

However, 1984 Convention is binding on States who submit themselves to it. The system of checks on observance of the convention-is weak and optional. A State ratifying the convention may elect not to be subject to verification' by 'opting out' of the relevant provisions of the Convention.

India has not so far acceded to the Convention Against Torture. In a letter to the Prime Minister, the then Chairman of the National Human Rights Commission, Justice Ranganath Misra, had urged that India should accede to the Convention against Torture and this is the "greatest, tribute" the country can pay to Mahatma Gandhi, Father of the Nation, on his 125th birth anniversary. The Prime Minister in his reply indicated that he shared the "feelings of the Commission".

However, in the Memorandum of Action Taken on the Annual Report of the National Human Rights Commission for the year (1994-95) the Ministry of Home Affairs stated that the question of India becoming, signatory to the Commission was discussed in the Chief Ministers' Conference held on 5/5/ 95 and the majority of the Chief Ministers were found either not in favour of the Convention or did not give their views. It was further stated in the Memorandum that as the Convention has to be implemented through the State agencies, due weightage to the views of the State Governments has to be given, and a decision in the matter will be taken after considering the views of all the State governments. This process will delay indefinitely India's accession to the Convention.

It is pertinent to note in this connection that torture has been made a punishable offencé under Sections 330 and 331 of the Indian Penal Code. Voluntarily causing hurt to extort confession or information is an offence under Section 330 IPC punishable with 7 years imprisonment and tine and 10 years imprisonment for causing grievous hurt under Section 331 IPC. Under 'Section 54 of the CrPC the accused person, if brought before a Magistrate can request a medical examination. This provision has been incorporated as a safeguard against torture. The Supreme Court in the case of *Francis Coralie Mullin v Union Territory of Delhi* (AIR 1981 SC 746) held that the expression right to life' in the Constitution means the right to live with basic dignity and hence torture or cruel, inhuman, degrading treatment which trenches on human dignity is not permissible under the Constitution. The Supreme Court has also upheld the right to compensation of the victims of torture in a number of cases.

Similarly, in quite a few cases of custodial violence NHRC has ordered payment of compensation to the victims of custodial violence and has further directed that this amount should be paid by the errant public servants themselves The Commission has suggested to the State governments to consider recovery of compensation amount from the offenders to bring about quicker sensitisation At its 1985 Session, the United Nations Commission on Human Rights welcomed the adoption by the General Assembly of the Convention against Torture and decided to appoint a Special Rapporteur to examine the various aspects of the question of torture. Peter H. Korjuman (Netherlands) was appointed as the Special Rapporteur and instructed to seek credible and reliable information concerning torture from governments, specialized agencies and to 'respond effectively' to such information. The Special Rapporteur in his report referred to practice of torture in many countries where a climate of violence has led to a disheartening loss of respect, for the physical and mental integrity of the human person and for his dignity. In this connection the report made special mention of the situation in Afghanistan and Sri Lanka. The report also recommended that introduction of a system of periodic visits by a committee of experts to places of detention or imprisonment will have a salutary preventive effect. Until such systems of periodic visits have been established, there should be granting of admission to International Committee of Red Cross (ICRC) teams to places of detention and imprisonment, as such visits by ICRC may contribute to prevention of torture, and, in fact, in some cases have ostensibly done so.

Remarkably, in his report to the United Nations Commission on Human Rights on his 1988 activities, the Special Rapporteur made some important recommendations. The report states that the great majority of allegations received by the Special Rapporteur refer to torture practised during incommunicado detention and hence a formal prohibition of incommunicado detention would greatly reduce the number of reported cases of torture. Further, the Code of Conduct for Law-enforcement officials and the Standard Minimum Rules for the Treatment of Prisoners should be translated into national languages and used as teaching materials during courses for law-enforcement officers, who should also be instructed on their duty to disobey orders received from a superior to practise torture.

The Commission on Human Rights on examination the reports of the Special Rapporteur endorsed most of his recommendations and conclusions and expressed their view that torture constitutes a criminal obliteration of human personality which can never be justified by any overriding circumstances or special ideology. The Vienna Declaration and Programme of Action was adopted by the World Conferences on Human Rights in June 1993. The World Conference on Human Rights welcomed ratification by many Member States of the Convention against Torture and other Cruel Inhuman Treatment or Punishment and encouraged speedy ratification by all other Member States.

The World Conference on Human Rights also reaffirmed that efforts to eradicate torture should first and foremost concentrate or prevention and therefore calls for early adoption of optional protocol to the Convention against Torture and other Cruel, Inhuman, Degrading Treatment or Punishment which is intended to establish a preventive treatment of regular visits to places 'of detention. The Conference further emphasizes that the State should abrogate legislation leading to impunity for those responsible for gross violation for human rights such as torture and prosecute such violations and thereby providing a firm basis for the rule of law. It may be mentioned in this connection that in West European countries there has been a remarkable progress in enforcing prohibition of torture. Article 3 of the European Convention on Human Rights contains a sweeping prohibition on torture. The European Commission Convention for the Prevention of Torture and Inhuman and Degrading Treatment or Punishment was open for signature in 1988. It went into force by 1989. By 1st of October, 1996, all the original 23 States of the Council of Western Europe have ratified it. All the new Member States in Central Europe, Albania, Bulgaria, Czech Republic, Hungary, Romania, Poland and Slovakia have also ratified -it.

The Committee of the Convention, CPT has one member per State. The work of the CPT is done by paying visits to the countries. The competence of the CPT is that they are allowed to inspect all places, where persons are kept against their will by the authorities like the police stations, prisons and mental asylums and interviewing persons in private if they so wish.

The European Human Rights Commission and the European Court of Human Rights in a number of cases held state parties responsible for acts of torture or inhuman treatment. In a famous case concerning, Turkey in 1976, the Commission concluded that the fact of not supplying enough food or water or medical treatment to the detainees in the zone of Cyprus under Turkish occupation amounted to inhuman treatment. In the famous Tyrer case the commission found the United Kingdom guilty of breach of article 3 of the European Convention on Human Rights and held that 'birching" of the juveniles as provided by law by British authorities in the Isle of Man is a degrading punishment, without any redeeming social value and is against article 3 of the European Convention.

In India, despite stringent laws and court rulings, torture and degrading treatment of citizens in various forms and manner continue to flourish. A study of the complaints received by NHRC shows that most of the victims of torture belong to poor and deprived classes. NHRC is also trying to closely monitor cases of custodial death and rape all over the country and asking the State governments to take corrective measures including stringent action against the aberrant staff.

India's accession to the Convention against Torture will be a step in the right direction and affirmation of the country's determination to do away with torture. This step will also send correct signals to the public servants, and particularly to the members of the police and security forces, not to transgress laws and rules of international conventions. The failure of the government to accede to the Convention has only provided a convenient handle to India's critics in international fora to severely indict it.

The Government of India has recently decided to accede to the Convention.

Culminating seven years of negotiating efforts, the United Nations General Assembly, on 10 December 1984, adopted by consensus the Convention against Torture and Other Cruel, Inhuman or Degrading Treatment or Punishment.

The Secretary-General of the United Nations, Javier Perez de Cuellar, noted on this occasion:

> "Surely one of the most insidious evils in this supposedly modern age is the continued practice of inflicting torture upon individual human beings. This Convention marks, therefore, an extremely important milestone in the continuing efforts of the United Nations to promote and ensure greater respect for human rights. The world community has thus outlawed once and for all the abominable practice of torture."

The subject has been of concern to the United Nations since early in its history. Articles providing that no one may be subjected to torture or to cruel, inhuman or degrading treatment or punishment were included in the Universal Declaration on Human Rights, adopted in 1948, and in the 1966 International Covenant on Civil and Political Rights. Other conventions-on genocide, *apartheid and* slavery for example—outlawed the practice for the groups to which those conventions pertained.

In fact, nine years before approving the new Convention, the General Assembly had adopted, on 9 December 1975, the Declaration on the Protection of All Persons from Being Subjected to Torture and Other Cruel. Inhuman or Degrading

Treatment or Punishment, condemning any act of torture as "an offence to human dignity", and laying down guidelines for all States and other entities exercising effective power. Two years later, the Assembly requested the Commission on Human Rights to study the question of torture and to draw up a draft Convention in the light of the principles contained in the Declaration. The Commission spent seven years preparing the text and, in March 1984, submitted the draft Convention to the General Assembly for adoption.

The Convention obliges States parties to prevent torture in their jurisdictions and to make torture a punishable offence. No circumstances-not war, not public emergency, not orders from a higher authority, nothing-can be invoked to justify torture. The treaty provides for extradition of torturers. Failing extradition, the State where the torturer is found shall prosecute him under certain conditions. This is an application of the exceptional concept of "universal penal jurisdiction" States parties also must provide for the right of victims to compensation and rehabilitation. To oversee implementation of the Convention, a Committee against Torture is to be set up.

The Committee is to consist of 10 experts of recognized competence in the human rights field elected by States parties to serve in their personal capacity, consideration being given to equitable geographical distribution. States parties will be required to report to the Committee every four years on measures they have taken to give effect to the Convention. Further, the Committee has the far-reaching power to examine *ex officio* reliable information alleging the systematic practice of torture in a State party, provided that the State party did not reject this provision upon ratification of the Convention.

If States make declarations under the appropriate articles

that they recognize the competence of the Committee to do so, the Committee may consider communications (under article 21) from one State party that another State party is not fulfilling its obligations under the Convention, or (under article 22) from individuals who claim to be victims of a violation of the Convention's provisions. At least five such declarations must be made before the provisions of either of those articles will enter into effect.

The Convention, which was open for signature on 4 February 1985, will enter into force 30 days after 20 States have ratified or acceded to it.

In addition to the efforts to eliminate torture, the United Nations has recognized the need to provide assistance to victims of torture in a purely humanitarian spirit; for this purpose the General Assembly established in 1981 the United Nations Voluntary Fund for Victims of Torture.

Torture continues to occur on a worldwide basis, despite enhanced efforts by Governments and organizations in keeping with provisions contained in domestic law and international human rights conventions whose objective is its total eradication.

The practice of torture was first prohibited in 1948 by the Universal Declaration of Human Rights and by the International Convention on the Prevention and Punishment of the Crime of Genocide; the concept was reaffirmed in 1966 by the International Covenant on Civil and Political Rights; and more recently, in 1984, by the Convention against Torture and Other Cruet, Inhuman or Degrading Treatment or Punishment.

The effects of torture should not be under-estimated. Physical and mental consequences of torture can endure for several years and may be irreversible, often affecting not only thousands of victims themselves, but also their relatives. One of the means of mitigating the subsequent effects of torture on victims and their families is to provide them with medical, psychological, social, legal and economic aid. With this in mind, the General Assembly' created the United Nations Voluntary Fund for Victims of Torture in 1982. The purpose of the Fund is to receive voluntary contributions and distribute them to non-governmental organizations and treatment centres for assisting victims of torture and their relatives whose human rights have been severely violated as a result of torture, as well as for the funding of projects for training health care professionals specialized in the treatment, of victims of torture.

The Fund is administered by the United Nations Secretary-General with a Board of Trustees acting in an advisory capacity and comprising five members with wide experience in the field of human rights. The members serve in their personal capacity and are appointed by the Secretary-General for a renewable three-year term of office on the basis of equitable geographical distribution. Currently, members of the Board of Trustees are Jaap Walkate. Chairman, from The Netherlands; Ribot Hatano from Japan; Elizabeth Odio-Benito from Costa Rica; Ivan Tosevsky from the Former Yugoslav Republic of Macedonia; and Amos Wako from Kenya.

The inadequacy of available resources is a limiting factor in the field of assistance to victims; as a consequence, programmes of assistance are subjected to interruptions. For some 100 organisations the support of the United Nations Voluntary Fund remains essential. During its sixtieth session, held in May 1997, the Board of Trustees examined 143 proposals for projects from 70 countries to be funded. The Board recommended that US$ 3,036,854 be allocated.

The High Commissioner fir Human Rights approved the recommendations of the Board on behalf of the Secretary-General. 20 new projects were launched and 104 projects were financed worldwide: 14 in North America, 21 in Central and South America, 30 in Western Europe, 10 in Eastern Europe, 14 in Africa, 15 in Asia, Oceania and the Middle East-It is important to note that the grants allocated to organizations based in North America and Western Europe are used for the treatment of as asylum-seekers and refugees victims of Torture coming from other regions of the world. It is a known fact that at least 50% of asylum-seekers and refugees who have been detained in their country of origin have been subjected to one or more forms of torture. The Fund receives projects which focus on providing medical, psychological, economic, social and legal assistance to victims of torture and to members of their families.

A few projects also share the objective of organizing training seminars for health professionals specialized in the treatment of torture victims. Each May, the Board of Trustees makes recommendations on grants to the High Commissioner for Human Rights. Subsequently, in the following month, on the basis of those recommendations, the High Commissioner takes decisions on behalf of the Secretary-General. As a final step, grants are made available at the end of July.

From 1983 to July 1997, the Fund has financed 255 projects for direct assistance to torture victims. From US$ 2,5 to US$ 3 million of voluntary contributions received from about 30 Governments and a few individuals are disbursed every year to projects in some 60 countries representative of all the regions of the world. Further information on the activities of the Voluntary Fund can be found in the latest annual reports of the Secretary-General to the General Assembly and to the Commission on Human Rights. Torture involves not only physical but also psychological forms, sometimes with long-term sequelae: in this regard, the Fund is supporting a project whose objective is to provide global assistance to formerly disappeared children of victims of torture in Latin America. The organization identifies disappeared children as those born in detention, abducted by security forces and illegally adopted. Once located by the organization, the children may be returned to their biological families. The best interests of the child have to be taken into consideration.

This project consists of two main parts: investigation - some 1,030 interviews were carried out in the past year in conjunction with blood tests and analyses of genetic data - and psychological support provided to some 43 1 persons during 1996. Most of these persons suffer from sequelae of post-traumatic stress disorder including anxiety, nightmares, depression, as well as affective and intellectual inhibitions and benefit from individual psychotherapy. The number of youths seeking assistance remains high while many children have yet to be found: to date, 172 children still need to be located and 6 who were found have yet to be returned to their biological families. Another project which was being implemented in Asia in 1996 focused on providing physical and mental relief to torture survivors and their families.

Firstly, fact-finding missions on the incidence of torture were carried out establishing that people had been subjected to torture by the police and other law enforcement agencies: this involved methods such as beatings all over the body, kicking them with police boots, applying electric shocks, scalding them with hot water, suspending them by the legs from roofs and inflicting them with bullet injuries. Long-term consequences, apart from obvious physical complaints, were psychological and included phobia, depression, sexual problems and mental disorders. The more commonly occurring complaints were social maladjustments at work, in the family and society in general, through the overall loss of social dignity and a departure from social values.

In 1995,263 victims between 15 and 45 years of age received treatment. The drug therapy included prescription of antipsychotics, physiotherapy as well as psychotherapeutic assistance. Parallel to the main objective of providing physical and mental relief to the victims, the Care Center organized other activities such as seminars on torture for health professionals, missions in collaboration with the national Human Rights Commission in order to establish contact with victims, encourage them to visit the Care Center and prepare a report for submission to governmental authorities asking for justice. The organization also established a legal division which has already successfully assisted in five cases. In North America, a treatment centre is currently providing clinical services to victims of torture who are now refugees, mainly from Africa and the Carribean. 167 persons were assisted who had been subjected to rape, electric shocks, deprivation of human needs, as well as being obliged to eat excrement, or perform acts of violence or murder often targeting their own family members.

The treatment provided ranges from psychiatric and medical examination, to treatment in the form of crisis intervention and support counselling, psychotherapy, physiotherapy, social service, education, medical referrals, social support interpreters and legal assistance. In 1996, the center also established a children's art therapy branch as a medium for treating anxiety and dysfunctions related to traumatic experiences which children were unable to express verbally in the family setting. The Commission on Human

Rights, by its resolution 1997/38 of 11 April 1997, requested that the General Assembly proclaim 26 June a United Nations international day in support of the victims of torture and appealed to all Governments, organizations and individuals in a position to do so to contribute annually to the fund.

The Committee Against Torture

The eradication of the practice of torture in the world was one of the major challenges taken up by the United Nations only a few years after its establishment. In order to ensure adequate protection for all persons against torture and other cruel, inhuman or degrading treatment or punishment, over the years the United Nations has adopted universally applicable standards. These standards were ultimately embodied in international declarations and conventions. The adoption on 10 December 1984 by the General Assembly of the United Nations of the Convention against Torture and Other Cruel, Inhuman or Degrading Treatment or Punishment rounded off the codification process to combat the practice of torture.

In developing this valuable instrument, the United Nations did not merely put in writing in a series of articles a body of principles and pious hopes, the implementation and observance of which would not be guaranteed by anything or anyone. It set up also a monitoring body, the Committee against Torture, whose main function is to ensure that the Convention is observed and implemented. The Committee met for the first time in April 1988 in Geneva and has since carried out intensive activities which, although often discreet, should make it known to the public at large.

The Convention against Torture and Other Cruel, Inhuman or Degrading Treatment or Punishment was adopted on 10 December 1984 by the General Assembly of the United

Nations, Consisting of 33 articles, this instrument, which 58 States had ratified or acceded to as of I January 1992, entered into force on 26 June 1987.

The Committee against Torture was established pursuant to article 17 of the Convention and began to function on 1 January 1988.

Here in this book we have taken the theme of human rights violations, its different patterns, magnitude and presented the statutory measures to curb such offences. Amply supported by case studies, statutes and judgments and other evidences the text is presented in comprehensive yet scientific analytic manner.

First we will take 'torture' and explain it from the human rights angle.

2

Torture: A Stigma on Civil Society

> "I think I could turn and live with animals, they are so placid and self-contained; I stand and look at them long and long. They do not sweat and whine about their condition; they do not lie awake in the dark and weep for their sins; not one is dissatisfied; not one is demented with the mania of owning things."
>
> —*Walt Whitman*

Moral and legal judgements regarding "cruelty" that derive from Art. 5 of the Universal Declaration of Human Rights (UDHR) have an interesting history in the West. The thesis that the universal rules enshrined in the Declaration cover a wide range of qualitatively different kinds of behaviour. First, that the modern history of 'torture' is not only a record of the progressive prohibition of cruel, inhuman and degrading practices. It is also part of a more complex story of the modern secular concept of what it means to be truly human. The second, the phase 'torture or cruel, in human or degrading treatment' serves today as a cross-cultural criterion for making moral and legal judgements about pain and suffering. Yet it is given much of its operative sense historically and culturally. Third the new ways of conceptualising suffering (a term that now refers also to non-humans, and even to the natural environment) are increasingly universal in scope but particular in prescriptive content. The final point is that the modern dedication to eliminating pain and suffering often conflicts with Other commitments and values: the right of individuals to choose, and the duty of the state to maintain its interests. Together, these four points aim at underscoring the unstable character of a central category deployed in modem, western society. The instability relates, in brief, to the fact that the ideas of torture, cruelty, inhumanity and degrading treatment are intended to measure what are often incommensurable standards of behaviour. In addition, they are applied in particular cases in a contradictory fashion.

Torture: A Backdrop

To begin, with, a discussion of two books show very different ways of writing histories of cruelty. The first, by G.R. Scott, represents physical cruelty as a feature of 'barbaric' societies - that is, societies that have not yet been humanised. The other book is by Darius Rejali. It makes a distinction between two kinds of physical cruelty, one appropriate to pre-modem and the other to modem societies, and describes that difference in the context of contemporary Iran. Scott was a Fellow of several British learned societies, including among them the Royal Anthropological Institute. Scott's (1940) History of Torture is perhaps the first modern story of its kind. It deals at length with 'Savage and Primitive Races', ancient and early modem European peoples, and Asian 'civilisations' (China, Japan and India).

On the one hand it tells a story of punishments now largely discontinued or suppressed; on the other it speaks of motives for inflicting suffering that are deep-rooted and pervasive. His indebtedness to Krafft-Ebing's ideas is evident not only in explicit form in his chapters on 'Sadism' and Masochism', but also in the general evolutionary scheme he employs according to which the primitive urge to inflict pain remains a latent possibility (sometimes realised) in civilised society. Scott is somewhat unusual for his time in wanting to include the mistreatment of animals in his account of torture, and in describing their plight as a consequence of the non-recognition of rights, for like other moderns he sees the extension of rights to be crucial for the elimination of cruelty.

But in the course of arguing this thesis he hits on a profound and disturbing ambiguity. It is not entirely clear whether he thinks that human cruelty is merely an instance of bestial cruelty - that is a working out of the supposedly universal instinct of stronger animals to hunt or attack the weaker, or whether human cruelty is unique - not a characteristic of animal behaviour at all -and that everyday human ruthlessness towards animals is essential for justifying the persecution of vulnerable people (defeated enemies, uninitiated children, etc.) on the grounds that they are not fully human, In either case Scott disturbs liberal ideas of what it is to be truly human: humans are essentially no different from other animals, or they are different by virtue of their unique capacity for cruelty.

It is worth noting that the instances of physical pain Scott describes as 'torture' belong sometimes to the involuntary submission for punishment and sometimes to the practices of personal discipline (for example, rituals of endurance, asceticism). Scott makes no distinction between the two: pain is regarded as an isolable experience to be condemned for what it is. In the encounter between 'Savage Rates' and modern Euro-Americans, Scott has no doubt that 'torture' is something the former do to the latter - perhaps because it is synonymous with 'barbarity'. At any rate the suffering inflicted on Native Americans by white settlers and the expanding US state has no place in his history of torture. This is not to say that Scott asserts torture to be entirely absent in the modem state. On the contrary, he is quite explicit about its use by the police to secure confession ('the third degree'). His position is that the story of modernity is in part a story of the progressive elimination of all morally shocking social behaviour - including what is now described in international law as 'cruel, inhuman and degrading treatment or punishment'. Scott does not claim that intention has been fully realised, only that progress has been made. In this story of progress, he tells us, the state's definition and defence of rights is the most effective protection against cruelty.

In his important book, the Iranian political scientist Darius Rejali (1994) makes the interesting argument that, far from being a barbaric survival in the modern state as Scott's story suggests, torture is in fact integral to it. Although he classifies torture into two types, modern and pre-modern, he shares with Scott the view that the term 'torture' has a fixed referent. More precisely, both of them assume that to speak of torture is to refer to a practice in which the agent forcibly inflicts pain on another regardless of the place that the practice occupies within a larger moral economy. Rejali offers a sophisticated account of the role of political punishments in Iran both before and after the inception of modernisation in that country. Modem torture, he tells us, is a form of physical suffering that is an inseparable part of a disciplinary society. In Iran the practice of torture is as essential to the Islamic Republic today as it was to the Pahlavi regime it replaced.

Both in their own way are modem disciplinary societies. Rejali believes that his book refutes what Foucault (1979) had to say about torture in Discipline and Punish. He maintains that torture does not replace discipline in modem society, as Foucault claimed, but persists in a major way. But this belief arises from a misreading of Foucault, whose central concern was not with 'torture' but with 'power': and consequently with a contrast between sovereign power (which needs to exhibit itself publicly) and disciplinary power (which works through the normalisation of everyday behaviour).

Public rituals of torture are no longer deemed to be necessary to the maintenance of sovereign power (whether they were in fact functionally necessary to the maintenance of "social order' is, of course, another question). But Foucault's thesis about disciplinary power is not subverted by evidence of surreptitious torture in the modern state. On the contrary, precisely because torture carried out in secret is intimately connected with the extraction of information, it is an aspect of policing. Policing is a governmental activity directed at defending a fundamental interest of society': the ordinary and extraordinary security of the state and its citizens.

It is also an institution in which knowledge and power depend upon each other, and where power - and this point is curiously neglected by Rejali -circulates in secret. Modem torture as part of policing is typically secret partly because inflicting physical pain on a prisoner to extract information, or for any purpose whatever, is 'uncivilised' and therefore illegal. It is also secret because policing agents do not wish to advertise everything they learn from tortured prisoners. After all, the effectiveness of certain kinds of disciplinary knowledge depends upon its secrecy. The secret character of knowledge acquired in policing therefore relates at once to the uncertainty of outside critics as to whether, and if so how often, something illegal has been done by a bureaucratic power to obtain it ('torture is intolerable in a civilised society"), and also to how, when and where law-enforcing power chooses to act once it possesses that secret information ('every society must protect itself against criminal conspiracies'). Rejali's definition of torture as 'sanguinary violence condoned by public authorities' slips uneasily between the legitimate and public practice of classical torture on the one hand, and, on the other, the secret because 'uncivilised' character of policing torture in modernising states like Iran. His fuller argument does not address this difference. Modem torture, he insists at length, is integral to what Foucault called disciplinary society. It is, if not itself quite identical with discipline, then very close to it. There are valuable insights in Rejali's book relating to the brutalising aspect of the process of modernisation. Here only two objections that might be made to his argument.

The first is that his main example (twentieth-century Iran) relates to what many readers will identify as a 'modernising' rather than a 'fully modem' society. Whether all the transformations in Iran in the period covered by Rejali's book truly represent modernisation in the sense of moral improvement is - these readers will say - an open question, but shocking evidence of blatant torture in that country does not prove that torture is integral to modernity. Rejali's argument at this point would have been stronger if he had referred to a modem society, like Nazi Germany, rather than a society on the way to being modernised. For although Nazi Germany was notoriously an illiberal state, it was certainly no less modem than any other.

The other objection is this: Rejali does not explain why, unlike discipline, modem state use of torture requires the rhetoric of denial. The brief answer to this question, surely, is that there is now a new sensibility regarding physical pain. Although it occurs frequently enough in our time, the modern conscience regards the inflicting of pain without 'good reason' (to perform a medical operation, say) as reprehensible, and therefore as an object of moral condemnation. It is this attitude to pain that helps define the modem notion of cruelty. The modem conscience is also a secular conscience, a category that subsumes what we now know as modem religion. Christianity, which was traditionally rooted in the doctrine of Christ's passion, consequently finds it difficult to make good sense of suffering today. Modern theologians have begun to concede that pain is essentially and entirely negative. 'The secularist challenge', writes a modem Catholic theologian:

> "even though separating many aspects of life from the religious field, brings with it a more sound, interpretive equilibrium; the natural phenomena, even though sometimes difficult to understand, have their cause and roots in processes that can and must be recognised. It is man's job, therefore, to enter into this cognitive analysis of the meaning of suffering, in order to be able to affront and conquer it.... Through his works, even before his words, Jesus of Nazareth proclaimed the goodness of life and of health, as the image of salvation. For Him pain is negativeness".

The writer in this passage is clearly thinking of disease, but since pain can also be a consequence of human intention, it follows that such pain should be eliminated from the world of human interaction - even from religious disciplines, and from the enactment of martyrdom, where it once had an effective and honoured place. The secular Christian must now abjure passion and choose action. Pain is not merely negativeness. It is, literally, a scandal.

Averting Torture

Why has the infliction of physical pain now become

scandalous?: A well-known part of the answer is this progressivist story: two centuries ago critics of torture like Beccaria and Voltaire recognised how inhuman it was, and how unreliable as a way of ascertaining the truth in a trial. Thus they saw and articulated what others before them had (unaccountably) failed to see. Their powerful case against judicial torture shocked Enlightenment rulers into abolishing it.

The theme of its intolerable cruelty emerged more clearly because the pain inflicted in judicial torture was declared to be gratuitous. Pain inflicted on prisoners to make them confess was immoral, it was argued, particularly because it was grossly inefficient in identifying their guilt or innocence. The Enlightenment reformers didn't necessarily condemn physical punishment as such, because it involved considerations other than simple instrumental ones, especially ideas of justice. Eventually, however, the evolution of modern ideas of justice were to contribute to growing hostility to painful punishment.

But why was this gratuitous pain not condemned by critics earlier? What had prevented people from seeing the truth until the Enlightenment? In his brilliant study Torture and the Law of Proof, John Langbein (1977) has provided a partial explanation. He demonstrates that torture was proscribed when the Roman canon law of proof - which required either confession or the testimony of two eyewitnesses to convict -declined in force in the seventeenth century. Increasing resort to circumstantial evidence secured convictions more easily and speedily. The abolition of judicial torture was thus in effect the moral condemnation and legal proscription of an extremely cumbersome and lengthy procedure that was now coming to be regarded as more or less redundant. Langbein implies that the moral truth about judicial torture was linked to the prior construction of a new concept of legal truth. When torture was the object of vigorous polemic in the eighteenth century, Jeremy Bentham came to the conclusion that the pain of torture is sometimes easier to justify than the suffering inflicted in the name of punishment. In the course of this justification he maintained, for example, that Courts of Law resorting to imprisonment in cases of contempt might find the application of physical pain, or even the threat of applying it, would secure obedience in a way 'less, penal' than prison:

> "A man may have been lingering in prison for a month or two before he would make answer to a question which at the worst with one stroke of the rack, and therefore almost always with only knowing that he might be made to suffer the rack, he would have answered in a moment; just as a man will linger on a Month with the Toothach [sic] which he might have saved himself from at the expense of a momentary pang".

It is not Bentham's apparent refusal to distinguish between voluntary and involuntary subjection to pain that should be noted here. It is the idea that subjective experiences of pain can be objectively compared. This idea is crucial for the modem understanding of 'cruel, inhuman and degrading treatment' in a cross-cultural context, although liberals today would strongly reject Bentham's view regarding the occasional preferability of torture to imprisonment.

For it is precisely some notion of comparability in suffering that makes of long years in prison (including solitary confinement) a "human' punishment and of flogging an 'inhumane' one, even though the experience of imprisonment and of flogging are qualitatively quite different. In an interesting passage in Discipline and Punish, Foucault (1979:

232) notes that in the nineteenth century imprisonment was compared favourably to other forms of legal punishment mainly because it was regarded as the, most egalitarian. This was a consequence of the philosophical doctrine that freedom was the natural human condition. Penal reformers reasoned that since the desire for liberty-was implanted equally in every individual, depriving individuals of their liberty must be a way of striking at them equally - that is, regardless of their social status or physical constitution. For just as fines were easier for the rich to pay, so physical pain could be borne better by the more sturdy.

No form of punishment accorded so precisely with our essential humanity, therefore, as imprisonment did. That legal incarceration was considered to be equitable contributed to the sense that physical punishment was gratuitous. For this reason, although modem liberals must regard Bentham wrong in the conclusion he reached about torture, they must consider him right to have endorsed a quantitative comparison of very disparate kinds of suffering. It is not difficult to see how the utilitarian calculus of pleasure and pain has come to be central to cross-cultural judgement in modem thought and practice. For by a reductive operation the idea of a calculus has facilitated the comparative judgement of what would otherwise remain incommensurable qualities.

Towards Humanising the World

The historical process of constructing a humane society, it is said, has aimed at eliminating cruelties. Thus it has often been observed that European rule in colonial countries, although not itself democratic, brought about moral improvements in behaviour - that is, the abandonment of practices that offend against the human. Major instruments in this transformation were modern legal, administrative and educational practices. And a central category deployed in them was the modern category of customary law. 'Of all the restrictions upon the application of customary laws during the colonial period', writes James Read (1972:175):

> the test of repugnancy 'to justice or morality' was potentially the most sweeping: for customary laws could hardly be repugnant to the traditional sense of justice or morality of the community which still accepted them, and it is therefore dear that the justice or morality of the colonial power was to provide the standard to be applied. Read points out that the phrase 'repugnant to justice and morality" does not have a precise legal meaning, and that early legislation in the colonies sometimes employed other expressions, such as 'not opposed to natural morality and humanity', to perform the same revolutionary work. But moral and social progress in those countries has been uneven. Although Europeans tried to suppress cruel practices and forms of suffering that were previously taken for granted in the non-European world by making the practitioners legally culpable, the suppression was not always completely successful. Today the struggle to eliminate social suffering is taken up by the United Nations. So the story goes.

However, in their attempt to outlaw customs the European rulers considered cruel, if was not the concern with indigenous suffering that dominated their thinking, but the desire to impose what they considered civilised standards of justice and humanity on a subject population—that is, the desire to create new human subjects. The anguish of subjects compelled under threat of punishment to abandon traditional practices - now legally branded as 'repugnant to justice and morality' or as 'opposed to natural morality and humanity", or even sometimes as 'backward and childish'—could not therefore play a decisive part in the discourse of colonial reformers.

On the contrary, as Lord Cromer (1913: 44) put it with reference to the misery created among the Egyptian peasantry by legal reforms under British rule: 'Civilisation must, unfortunately, have its victims.' In the process of learning to be 'fully human' only some kinds of suffering were seen as an affront to humanity, and their elimination sought. This was distinguished from suffering that was necessary to the process of realising one's humanity - that is, pain that was adequate to its end, not wasteful pain. Inhuman suffering, typically associated with barbaric behaviour, was a morally insufferable condition for which someone responsible; those requiring it (themselves inhuman enough to cause it to be inflicted) must be made to desist, and if necessary punished. That, at any rate, is the discourse of progressive reform. What individual colonial administrators actually felt, thought or did is another (though not entirely unrelated) matter. Most experienced administrators were prepared locally to tolerate various 'uncivilised' practices for reasons of expediency, but all were no doubt aware of the dominant progressivist discourse rooted in 'civilised' societies.

In a recent unpublished paper by Nicholas Dirks there is a lucid illustration of just this discourse in late nineteenth-century British India. His account of the inquiry conducted by the colonial authorities into the ritual of hook swinging contains this sober judgement by the presiding, British official:

> "It is, in my opinion, unnecessary at the end of the nineteenth century and, having regard to the level to which civilisation in India has attained, to consider the motives by which the performers themselves an actuated when taking part in hook swinging, walking through fire, and other barbarities. From their own moral standpoint, their motives may be good or they may be bad; they may indulge in self-torture in

> satisfaction of pious vows fervently made in all sincerity and for the most disinterested reasons, or they may indulge in it from the lowest motives of personal aggrandisement, whether for the alms they might receive or for the personal distinction and local eclat that it may bring them; but the question is whether public opinion in this country is not opposed to the external acts of the performers, as being in fact repugnant to the dictates of humanity and demoralising to themselves and to all who may witness their performances.
>
> I am of the opinion that the voice of India most entitled to be listened to with respect, that is to say, not only the voice of the advanced school that has received some of the advantages of western education and has been permeated with non-Oriental ideas, but also the voice of those whose views of life and propriety of conduct have been mainly derived from Asiatic philosophy, would gladly proclaim that the time had arrived for the Government in the interests of its people to effectively put down all degrading exhibitions of self-torture".

The fact that the performers themselves declared that they felt no pain was irrelevant. So, too, was the plea that this was a religious rite. Such claims to difference were not acceptable. It was the offence given by the performance to a particular concept of being human that reduced qualitatively different kinds of behaviour to a single standard. Confirmation of its offensiveness was obtained by listening to some colonised voices only. The latter included Indians who were directly westernised. But, more significantly, confirmation were provided also by those who accepted a westernised exegesis of their 'Asiatic philosophy". From the point of view of moral progress, the: voices of those who took up a reactionary position could not be attended to. Clearly, in the cause of moral progress there was suffering and suffering.

What is interesting, is not merely that some forms of suffering were to be taken more seriously than others, but that 'inhuman' suffering as opposed to 'necessary' or 'inevitable' suffering was regarded as being essentially gratuitous, and therefore legally punishable. Pain endured in the movement towards becoming 'full human', on the other hand, was necessary, in the sense that there were social or moral reasons why it had to be suffered. This view is of a piece with the post-Enlightenment concern to construct through judicial punishment the most efficient means of reforming offenders and of guarding society's interests. As the idea of progress became increasingly dominant in the affairs of Europe and the world, the need for measuring suffering was felt and responded to with greater sophistication.

Torture and Acting with Deliberate Cruelty

Pain is not always regarded as insufferable in modern Euro-American societies. In warfare, sport and psychological experimentation—as well as in the domain of sexual pleasure—inflicting physical suffering is actively practised and also legally condoned. This makes for contradictions which are exploited in public debate. When transitive Pain is described as 'cruel and inhuman' it is often referred to as torture. And torture itself is condemned by public opinion and prohibited by international law. It is hardly surprising, therefore, that the many liberal-democratic governments that have employed torture have attempted to do so in secret. And sometimes they have been concerned to redefine legally the category of pain-producing treatment in an attempt to avoid the label 'torture'. Thus:

> Torture is forbidden by Israeli law. Israeli authorities say that torture is not authorised or condoned in the occupied territories but acknowledge that abuses occur and state that they

> are investigated. In 1987 the Landau judicial Commission specifically condemned 'torture' but allowed for 'moderate physical and psychological pressure' to be used to secure confessions and to obtain information; a classified annex to the report defining permissible pressure has never been made public. Needless to say, other governments in the region (for example, Egypt, Turkey and Iran) have also condoned torture and, unlike liberal-democratic governments, they have used it freely against their own citizens. But the remarkable feature of this case is the scrupulous concern of a liberal-democratic state with calibrating the amount of pain that is legally allowable. There is evidently a concern that too much pain should not be applied. It is assumed that 'moderate physical and psychological pressure' is at once necessary and sufficient to secure confession. Beyond that quantity, pressure is held to be excessive (gratuitous), and therefore presumably becomes 'torture'. Other states in the Middle East are rarely so punctilious, or so modern in their reasoning.

The use of torture by liberal-democratic states relates to their attempt to control populations that are not citizens. In such cases torture cannot be attributed to 'primitive urges'- as Scott suggested. Nor to governmental techniques for disciplining citizens, as Rejali has argued. It is to be understood as a practical logic integral to the maintenance of the nation-state's sovereignty, like warfare.

The category of torture is no longer limited to applications of physical pain: it now includes psychological coercion in which disorientation, isolation and brainwashing are employed. Indeed 'torture' in our day functions not only to denote behaviour actually prohibited by law, but also desired to be so prohibited in accordance with changing concepts of Inhumane' treatment (for example, the public execution or flogging of criminals, and child abuse, as well as animal experiments, factory farming and fox hunting). This wider category of torture, or 'cruel, inhuman and degrading treatment', could in theory be applied to the anguish and mental suffering experienced by people in societies obliged to give up their beliefs and 'become fully human'.

Remarkably, by a curious paradox it is a version of relativism that prevents such an application of the category. For the anguish is itself the consequence of a passionate investment in the Truth of beliefs that guide behaviour. The modern sceptical posture, in contrast, regards such passionate conviction to be 'uncivilised', as well as a perpetual source of danger to others and of pain to oneself. Beliefs should either have no direct connection to the way one lives, or be held so lightly that they can be easily changed. One might be inclined to think that at least in humanising societies more sorts of inflicted pain come to be considered morally unacceptable with the passage of time. In some cases, however, pain-producing behaviour that was once shocking no longer shocks. Or if it does, then not in the way it did in the past. Putting large numbers of people in prison for more and more kinds of offence is one example. Inflicting new forms of suffering in battle is another.

Some writers on pain such as Elaine Scarry (1985:61) have claimed that war is 'the most obvious analogue to torture'. However that may be, it is significant that the general concept of 'cruel, inhuman and degrading treatment or punishment' is not applied to the normal conduct of war -although modem, technological warfare involves forms of suffering, in numbers and in kind, that are without precedent.

The Geneva Convention, it is true, seeks to regulate conduct in war. But paradoxically, this has the effect of legalising most of the new kinds of suffering endured in modern war by combatants and noncombatants alike. The military historian John Keegan (1978) wrote of the new practices of 'deliberate cruelty' nearly two decades ago when he described some of the weaponry employed in twentieth-century warfare:

> "Weapons have never been kind to human flesh, but the directing principle behind their design has usually not been that of maximising the pain and damage they can cause. Before the invention of explosives, the limits of muscle power in itself constrained their hurtfulness; but even for some time thereafter moral inhibitions, fuelled by a sense of the unfairness of adding mechanical and chemical increments to man's power to hurt his brother, served to restrain deliberate barbarities of design. Some of these inhibitions - against the use of poison gas and explosive bullets - were codified and given international force by the Hague Convention of 1899;17 but the rise of 'thing-killing" as opposed to man-killing weapons - heavy artillery is an example - which by their side-effects inflicted gross suffering and disfigurement, invalidated these restraints. As a result restraints were cast to the winds, and it is now a desired effect of many man-killing weapons that they inflict wounds as terrible and terrifying as possible. The claymore mine, for instance, is filled with metal cubes... the cluster bomb with jagged metal fragments, in both cases because that shape of projectile tears and fractures more extensively than a smooth-bodied one. The HEAT and HESH rounds fired by anti-tank guns are designed to fill the interior of armoured vehicles with showers of metal splinters or streams of molten metal, so disabling the tank by disabling its crew. And napalm, disliked for ethical reasons even by many tough minded soldiers, contains an ingredient

> which increases the adhesion of the burning petrol to human skin surfaces. Military surgeons, so successful over the past century in resuscitating wounded soldiers and repairing wounds of growing severity, have thus now to meet a challenge of wounding agents of growing deliberately conceived to defeat their skills."

One might add to this that the manufacture, possession and deployment of weapons of mass destruction (chemical, nuclear and biological) must be counted as instances of declared governmental readiness to engage in 'cruel, inhuman, and degrading treatment' against civilian populations even when they are not actually used. In brief, cruel modem technologies of destruction are integral to modern welfare, and modern welfare is an activity essential to the security and power of the modem state, on which the welfare and identity of its citizens depends. In war, the modern state demands from its citizens not only that they kill and maim others but also that they themselves suffer cruel pain and death. So how can the calculated cruelties of modern battle be reconciled with the modern sensibility regarding pain? Precisely by treating pain as a quantifiable essence.

As in state torture, an attempt can be made to measure the physical suffering inflicted in modern warfare in accordance with the proportionality of means to ends. The human destruction inflicted should not outweigh the strategic advantage gained. But given the aim of ultimate victory the notion of 'military necessity' can be 'extended indefinitely. Any measure that is intended as a contribution to that aim, no matter how much suffering it creates, may be justified in terms of 'military necessity". The standard of Acceptability in such cases is set by public opinion, and that standard varies as the latter moves in response to contingent circumstances.

Subjection to 'Cruel and Degrading Treatment'

It is pertinent to note that while the category of 'torture' has in recent times been expanded to include cases of induced suffering that are primarily or entirely psychological, it has also been narrowed to exclude some cases of the calculated infliction of physical pain. This sometimes leads to contradictions. But there is another kind of contradiction which is characteristic of modern social life. Modern are aware of situations in which the sharp separation between the negative experience of pain and the positive experience of pleasure are inseparable. Sadomasochism is disturbing to many people precisely because here they are confronted with suffering that is no longer simply painful. It is at once pain and the opposite of pain. Two centuries of powerful criticism directed at the Utilitarians; calculus of pleasure versus pain has not destroyed the commonsense view that these two experiences should be mutually exclusive. Yet in the eroticisation of suffering the two are intimately linked, and it is actively sought by some.

Here is an extract from a sadomasochist text *The Leatherman's Handbook II* (Townsend 1989):

> "Because I consider any attempt to define SM in a single concise phrase to be the ultimate exercise in futility—or masochism—I shall forego the temptation to add yet another version to the great discarded stack of unsuccessful, inadequate verbal garbage. Instead let me suggest a short list of characteristics I find to be present in most scenes which I would classify as SM:
>
> 1) A dominant-submissive relationship.
> 2) A giving and receiving of pain that is pleasurable to both parties.
> 3) Fantasy and/or role playing on the part of one or both partners.

4) A conscious humbling of one partner by the other (humiliation).
5) Some form of fetish involvement.
6) The acting out of one or more ritualised interactions (bondage, flagellation, etc.)."

Notice that this text speaks not about expressions of pain, still less about conventional play-acting, but about pain experienced and inflicted, in which both partners, the active and the passive, are jointly agents. So why is sadomasochism not rejected by all modern who condemn pain as a negative experience? One answer, according to some interpreters, is that not everyone social confuses the distinction between unbridled sadism and the social subculture of consensual fetishism. To argue that in consensual S/M the 'dominant' has power, and the slave has not, is to read theatre for reality'.

However the point of my question is not to dismiss the distinction between/unbridled sadism' and the subculture of consensual fetishism,. It is to ask what happens when individual self-fashioning embraces every difference -including the difference between 'pain' and 'pleasure, - within an aesthetic whole. We are sometimes told that the hybridisation of categories, including those that organise our sensual experience, is a mode by which stable authority may be subverted in the name of liberty. But it is possible also that the eroticisation of pain is merely one of the ways in which the modern self attempts to secure its elusive foundation. Recently, an article in a London newspaper gave the following account of a local performance by an American artist at the Institute of Contemporary Arts (ICA):

> "With his face set in a mask of concentration, Ron Athey allows his head to be pierced with a six-inch

> needle just above the eyebrow. You watch, transfixed, as needle snakes along beneath the skin like water pulsing through an empty hosepipe. A droplet of blood wells up at the point where steel meets scalp. This is the first spike of Athey's crown of thorns - a body piercer's tribute to the power of Christian, iconography, an ex-junkie's flirtation with the needle, and a gay man's defiance of infection with HIV.

By the time the macabre 'sketch' is finished, Athey is encrusted with needles, garlanded with wire and oozing blood, in what appears to be a parody of the crucifixion. Ah, but is it a parody, defined in the dictionary as 'an imitation so poor as to seem a deliberate mockery of the original'? Or is it -as Athey's supporters would claim - an exploration of the nature of martyrdom, as manifest to a worldwide gay community in the era of Aids" ?

What is remarkable about these statements is that the writer of this account finds herself having to put the familiar theatrical word 'sketch' in quotation marks - but not so the equally familiar theological expression 'martyrdom'. The reader is given to understand that this is a real tribute to the power of Christian iconography, a real exploration of the nature of (Christian) martyrdom, but that it only 'appears' to be a form of theatre, an 'imitation'.

In the discourse of modem self-fashioning, the tension holding 'real, and 'theatrical' apart can collapse. It is especially in a modern culture, where the split between the real and its mere representation has become institutionalised, that it becomes necessary to assert from time to time that a given performance is merely theatrical, or that another performance is not really theatre. The point here, however, is that it is the difference between 'the real' and 'the mimetic' - like the difference between 'pain' and 'pleasure' - that is available to modern self-fashioning. And that consequently the tension between 'real' and 'pretend' bondage is itself aestheticised, and the clear distinction between consent and coercion problematised of course S/M as defined in the text is different from this performance at the ICA.

For one thing, in the latter there is a separation between performers and observers. No experience of giving and receiving pain binds the two together in mutual pleasure. We find only a one-sided representation (presentation?) of an evocative image of suffering, which is preceded by a painful construction of that image on the stage. Furthermore, its intention is not the production of private pleasure. We can't know whether the various members of Athey's audience respond primarily to the icon of Christ's last passion, or to the painful construction of that icon on the stage - or to both. Nor can we tell what difference it would make to those who would like to ban this performance if they were to be told that Athey suffers from a malfunctioning of the nervous system so that he actually feels no pain. Or - more tellingly - that like a religious virtuoso he-has learnt to experience it positively.

Think of the Shi'a Muslim flagellants mourning the martyrdom of the Prophet's grandson Hussain annually every Muharram. That instance of self-inflicted pain is at once real and dramatic (not 'theatrical'). It has even less to do with 'pleasure' than does Athey's performance. It differs from the latter in being a collective rite of religious suffering and redemption. It is not a secular act that borrows a religious metaphor to make a political statement about prejudice. Nor is it premised on the right to self-fashioning and the autonomy of individual choice. Yet both strike against the modern sensibility that recoils from a willing, positive engagement with suffering. Because for ascetics, as for sadomasochists, pain is not merely a means which can be measured and pronounced excessive or gratuitous in relation to an end. Pain is not action but passion.

These brief references to pain willingly endured in modem society help us to raise some questions at the transcultural level.

The interesting thing about the criteria enumerated in the S/M text is that they come up against Article 5 of the Universal Declaration of Human Rights: 'No one shall be subjected to torture or to cruel, inhuman or degrading treatment or punishment.' This rule is not qualified by the phrase 'unless the parties concerned are consenting adults'. In the same way, and for the same reason, one may not consent to sell oneself into slavery, even for a limited period, and not even if the parties concerned find the relationship of bondage erotic.

So, too, the liberalised Church strongly disapproves of monks being whipped at the command of their abbot for penalisable faults - even when the penance has a ritual closure and a dramatic character. And even if the monks have taken monastic vows of obedience voluntarily. This follows from the modern rejection of physical pain in general, and of 'gratuitous' suffering in particular. But it is more precise to put it this way: the modem hostility is not simply to pain, it is to pain that does not accord with a particular conception of being human - and that is therefore in excess. 'Excess' is a concept of measure. An essential aspect of the modem attitude to pain rests on a calculus that defines appropriate actions.

The concern however, is with the structure of public debate over the valorisation of painful experience in a culture that regards it negatively. In that debate argument is sharpened because, oh the one hand, modems disapprove of physical pain as 'degrading". On the other hand they are committed to every individual's right to pursue unlimited physical pleasure 'in private'- so long as that conforms to the legal principle of consenting adults and does not lead to death or serious injury. Thus one way that modems attempt to resolve this contradiction is by defining cruelty in relation to the principle of individual autonomy, which is the necessary basis of free choice. However, if the concept of 'cruel, inhuman and degrading treatment' cannot be consistently deployed without reference to the principle of individual freedom, it becomes relativised.

This becomes clearer in the transcultural domain. For here it is not simply a matter of eliminating particular cruelties, but of imposing an entire modern discourse of 'being human', central to which are its ideas about individualism and detachment from passionate belief. Thus while at home the principle of consenting adults within the bounds of the law works by invoking the idea of free choice based on individual autonomy, the presence of consenting adults abroad may often be taken to indicate mere 'false consciousness'- a fanatical commitment to outmoded beliefs - which invites forcible correction.

Yet only the suspicious individual - suspicious of others and of herself - can be truly autonomous, truly free of fanatical convictions. But continuous suspicion introduces instability at another level: that of the subject.

It has been tried to problematise the basic idea underlying the United Nations declaration that 'No one shall be subjected to torture or to cruel, inhuman or degrading treatment or punishment' has been suggested that the idea instable mainly because the aspirations and practices to which it is attached are themselves-contradictory. Of course, the fact that an idea is unstable may not, in itself, be reason enough for abandoning it. But neither the attempt by Euro-Americans to impose their standards by force on others, nor the willing invocation of these standards by weaker peoples in the Third World, makes them stable or universal. It merely globalises them.

We need ethnographies of pain and cruelty which can provide us with a better understanding of how relevant practices are actually conducted in different traditions. Such ethnographies will certainly show us that cruelty can be experienced and 'addressed in ways other than as a violation of rights - for example, as a failure of specific virtues or as an expression of particular vices. They will also show us that if cruelty is increasingly represented in the language of rights' (and especially of human rights), then this is because perpetual legal struggle has now become the dominant mode of moral engagement in an interconnected, uncertain and rapidly changing world.

3

Patterns of Torture and Victims

> "A greater poverty than that caused by lack of money is the poverty of unawareness. Men and women go about the world unaware of the beauty, the goodness, the glories in it. Their souls are poor. It is better to have a poor pocketbook than to suffer from a poor soul."
>
> —*Thomas Dreier*

Torture is not only frequently reported in India, it has even been depicted in newspapers. In May 1991 the *Hindustan Times* published a photograph of a man apparently being tortured in a police station. The caption read: "... Here is Kailash Rai, a suspect, being given the 'aeroplane' treatment by a policeman in Baktiarpur police station.... Kailash bowed before the 'aeroplane' and is reported to have confessed to his being a mercenary hired for booth-capturing in the forthcoming elections in Bihar".

Many torture victims were arrested in connection with criminal investigations and tortured to extract information and confessions. Others were arrested because a relative or friend was sought by the police or because false charges were brought against them at the behest of powerful local interests - members of state ruling parties, businessmen or landowners. This is particularly common in states in which there is organized opposition to economic exploitation, such as Bihar, where the police appear often to act as an instrument of repression on behalf of local ruling groups. Torture is also widespread in areas where the government faces armed opposition -Jammu and Kashmir, Punjab, Assam and the northeast states - and regions of central India where the *Naxalites* are active. Here torture is a means of obtaining confessions and gathering intelligence, but it has an extra dimension: it is also used as a deterrent and in reprisal for attacks by armed groups.

The most common torture methods are severe beatings, sometimes while the victim is hung upside down, and electric shocks. People have also been crushed with heavy rollers, burned, stabbed with sharp instruments, and had objects such as chilies or thick sticks forced into their rectums. Sexual mutilation has been reported. Rape is a common form of torture. It is so routine that a *1988* newspaper headline read: "Another mass rape by Bihar cops" In September *1989* the Rajasthan state government admitted that the police had been involved in over 50 rapes in the past few years. According to the Delhi police, 14 cases of rape were reported involving 20 police officers at 12 police stations between *1* January and 11 February *1990*. Rape of women appears to be used by the police and the security forces to deter opposition and also as a means of indirectly punishing the men from a particular village or area, As an editorial in *The Statesman* commented, "the police abuse women to carry out a proxy war against what their menfolk stand for".

Almost all Amnesty International's information about torture and death in custody comes from within India itself. Amnesty international has regularly monitored Indian public information sources, including journals and newspapers. The organization has been denied access to India for research purposes by successive governments since *1984:* it has nevertheless obtained first-hand information from a variety of sources and evidence contained in medical and judicial records as well as sworn affidavits by the victims and witnesses to torture. Particularly important have been the findings of official commissions of inquiry into aspects of police behaviour and into specific allegations of abuse.

Independent civil liberties organizations have played a crucial role in monitoring and bringing to public attention cases of human rights violations. They have published the results of detailed on-the-spot investigations into torture, rape and death in custody. It is often only as a result of their work that a pattern of human rights violations can be documented, particularly in remote areas. These organizations include the Andhra Pradesh Civil Liberties Committee (APCLC); the Association for the Protection of Democratic Rights (APDR). Calcutta; the Civil Liberties and Human Rights Organization (CLAHRO) in Manipur; Citizens for Democracy (CFD), Delhi; the Committee for the Protection of Democratic Rights (CPDR), Bombay; the Free Legal Aid Committee (FLAC) in Bihar, the Jammu and Kashmir People's Basic Rights (Protection) Committee; the Naga People's Movement for Human Rights (NPMHR); the People's Union for Civil Liberties (PUCL); and the People's Union for Democratic Rights (PUDR).

Numerous cases of torture have been reported in the Indian news media but these represent only a fraction of the real total. Torture frequently goes unreported unless there is *an* investigation by an independent human rights or civil liberties body, some form of public protest, or a political dimension. Successive Indian governments have persistently refused to investigate the abuses documented in such reports and have frequently sought to discredit their authors. Some civil liberties activists have been detained because of their work. In exceptional cases the courts have taken action to prevent torture. The Guwahati High Court, which has jurisdiction over all seven northeast states, has taken significant steps to restrain the army from using torture and committing other human rights violations. In July *1991* the court suspended five police officers from Tripura accused of torturing detainees, and instructed the director general of police to initiate proceedings against them.

The court also ordered the immediate transfer of the officer in charge of the police station where the torture occurred and directed the state government not to confine any prisoners there. In July *1991* the Supreme Court declared that the army was under a duty to comply strictly with the requirements of the Code of Criminal Procedure when arresting or searching women. This ruling was delivered after newspapers reported that women were being harassed by members of the security forces in the northeast states Other Supreme Court judgments about female detainees, however, have been openly criticized. For example, in December *1989* the Supreme Court reduced by half the 10-year sentences passed on two police constables in Haryana who had been convicted of rape. The court's ruling was based on its assessment of the victim's character; it provoked much criticism, not least because it appeared to negate a *1983* amendment to the law on rape. This had introduced a minimum sentence of 10 years' imprisonment for any police officer convicted of custodial rape.?

Journalists who expose human rights violations have also been detained and ill-treated. Threats against journalists and assaults on them are frequently reported. In July 1989 Bramhadeo Singh Sharma, 84-year-old editor of Awaaz, a Hindi newspaper in Bihar, was dragged from his house by police and forced to remain standing for several hours. This occurred after he wrote an editorial condemning the police administration for failing to punish officers who had publicly stripped and beaten unconscious Malati Manjhiyan, a tribal teenage girl. He was released following protests by journalists and others. The seven police officers responsible, including the senior officer, were suspended but no further action is known to have been taken against them.

This case is just one which illustrates official failure to acknowledge that torture occurs. In November 1989 the United Nations (UN) Special Rapporteur on torture transmitted information about the case of Malati Manjhiyan to the Indian Government and sought its response. In 1991 the Supreme Court had upheld Malati Manjhiyan's claim for compensation and awarded her damages against the police but despite this, the government had still not responded to the UN by the end of 1990. The government's persistent failure to acknowledge that torture is routine serves to ensure that the established pattern of its practice throughout India will continue.

The Pattern of Torture

In May 1990 the Supreme Court quashed criminal charges against 28 men who had been awaiting trial in Bihar for over 10 years. This is the only case known to Amnesty International in which charges have been dropped against torture victims. It also ordered the release on parole of two others who had been sentenced to 20 years' imprisonment in 1987. The case was one of the best known because of the particularly cruel and inhuman torture inflicted on the accused, victims of the Bhagalpur blindings. At the end of the 1970s police in Bihar, faced with a steep rise in armed robbery carried out by gangs of young men, decided- to blind suspects as a deterrent to others. Over 30 men and boys were deliberately blinded with thick needles and acid between October 1979 and November 1980.

The youngest victim was 16 years old. Few of the 30 who were blinded had criminal records and, according to one commentator, no more than four had previously been charged with involvement in criminal activities. One victim, Suresh Sah, was apparently blinded as a punishment for refusing to work for low wages for local landlords. A police sub-inspector, a doctor and eight landlords were convicted in 1984 of a criminal conspiracy to blind him. The blindings were reported in the weekly magazine Sunday on 16 November 1980 and caused a public outcry. Indira Gandhi, then Prime Minister, said in parliament: "I want to convey my own deep agony at what has happened.... This is not just a question of punishment, we must make a major effort in the training of these forces whereby they do not become dehumanised". The victims were awarded compensation and rehabilitation and had their trials stayed by the Supreme Court, which immediately ordered medical examination of the victims, asked its own Registrar to investigate the case and asked the courts in Bihar why they had not proceeded against the accused police officers. The court ordered the Bihar state government to produce all relevant documents to clarify the involvement of state officials in the Windings. The Bihar government sought to disclaim responsibility on the grounds that its officers had acted outside the law.

The man who had been instrumental in exposing the Windings was the superintendent of Bhagalpur jail. He was suspended without pay in December 1980 for allegedly not revealing the full facts of the case. Yet, according to his petition to the Supreme Court appealing against his suspension, he had first reported the blinding of a prisoner in November 1979, when he sent a report to the chief judicial magistrate, urging him to carry out an investigation. He said' that he had repeatedly notified the authorities that prisoners awaiting trial in Bhagalpur jail had been deliberately blinded by the police. He said that he had taken the inspector general of prisons to interview three of the blinded prisoners but that the inspector general's subsequent demands for a full inquiry were ignored. The superintendent also said that the home commissioner, the Bihar minister for jails and other state officials were aware of the Windings but had made no attempt to prevent or investigate them. "In spite of the best possible efforts made by me as well as by., the then Inspector General of Prisons, Bihar, to bring the matter to the notice of the appropriate authorities so that they might take steps to prevent the recurrence of Windings, I found the local authorities as well as the state government insensitive towards the Winded and by now 31 suspects had been blinded."

The first inquiry was carried out by the deputy inspector general of the Bihar Criminal Investigation Department (CID). He was ordered to go to Bhagalpur to establish whether the police had carried out the Windings. He later said: "I was given the job because they knew that I had a great weakness for the police force...and they expected me to cover up. I went thinking that the police could never be guilty of such brutality, but after examining the victims for two days I got 32 cases instituted against 10 police officers". When his superiors received his first report, he alleged, his inquiries were promptly blocked. Nevertheless, he submitted a 70-page report to the Bihar government in December 1980, followed in January 1981 by separate reports on each case. On 10 February 1981 to vacate his office by the following day and was demoted. The next inquiry, carried out by the Central Bureau of Investigation (CBI) in January 1982, absolved the state government of complicity or negligence in the blindings. It found that they were isolated instances of crime without any conspiracy and recommended criminal prosecution in 10 cases, and departmental action in a further nine cases. The cases against the police officers proceeded very slowly through the courts. According to Amnesty International's information, the last case was heard in 1987. In all, nine police officers were convicted for their part in blinding just five of the prisoners. No senior officer was prosecuted, although the CBI had reported that at least one had prior knowledge of the blindings and did not act to prevent them.

Remarkably, the police windings in Bhagalpur illustrate key aspects of the pattern of torture in India: the sanction of torture by state and local judicial authorities, the routine concealment of torture, the failure to conduct proper inquiries, and the inordinate length of judicial proceedings - it was 10 years after the Windings that the Supreme Court quashed the charges against the victims. However, the case, is exceptional because a nationwide public outcry resulted in concern at the highest level of government and the prosecution and punishment of at least some of those responsible. Nevertheless, several of the police officers allegedly involved apparently escaped trial and the longest sentence served by a police officer convicted of deliberately blinding a prisoner was three years.

Torture of Criminal Suspects

Criminal suspects form a large proportion of India's torture victims. The most common purpose of torturing criminal suspects is to extract a confession, or to secure information about a crime, however petty the offence and irrespective of whether a crime has actually been committed. In April 1989 the Bombay High Court ordered a police investigation into the torture of four teenage girls by the

Maharashtra police. The four girls, all members of a nomadic tribe, had been charged with "moving about in a suspicious manner". Many victims of torture are jobless, slum-dwellers or migrant labourers who have come to the cities in search of work. Most victims of police rape in Delhi, for example, are migrant women, who often disappear after the rape because they are too frightened to pursue the matter. Even children as young as six have been arrested and tortured in connection with petty criminal offences.

In mid-1989 the press reported that a group of children and teenagers had been tortured in northwest Delhi. The children, all slum-dwellers, were detained on 26 June 1989 on suspicion of theft. The case was brought to public attention by two civil liberties groups, which reported that 11 children, including two 10-year-old girls and a boy aged six, had been illegally detained and tortured throughout the night. A girl of 13 had been stripped naked and beaten and one 12-year-old boy was given electric shocks and beaten with a leather belt; another boy was stripped, hung upside-down from the ceiling and beaten unconscious. The children were released the following day after a crowd of 4,000 people had gathered outside the police station.

Lawyers successfully petitioned the courts for the children to be given a medical examination. The publicity this case received forced the police to announce an inquiry, although the deputy commissioner of police denied that the police were responsible. He said the children had been "roughed up" by members of the family whose goods were stolen. The case was the subject of an inquiry to the Indian Government by the UN Special Rapporteur on torture and it was cited in his 1989 report 8, but as of the end of 1991 the government had not responded.

Torture to Punish Political Activism

There is also a pattern of torture and ill-treatment in punitive reprisals for resistance to police or military operations. In many Indian states the police have been accused of detaining and torturing people on false charges at the behest of influential local interests. For example, the Calcutta-based Telegraph reported in February 1990 that villagers from Rampur village, near Balagarh in West Bengal, said they had been tortured due to pressure from local members of the state ruling party, the Communist Party of India (Marxist). Apparently, a CPI(M) activist had lodged a false complaint of assault against a village leader who was a member of the rival Congress(I) party.

The police then took a number of villagers, including several women, into custody and reportedly tortured them at Balagarh police station: one victim was a 12-year old girl, Sabina Yasmeen. Another victim, Sheikh Abdul Wal, alleged: "The police beat me up black and blue saying I must riot dare to support the Congress again". The local deputy superintendent of police denied the allegations. In early September *1991* a Delhi policewoman was among several men and women detained and tortured after police raided the village of Barhi in Ballabgarh, Haryana. The raid was apparently in reprisal for an incident on 30 August, when police officers attempting to arrest villagers in connection with a land dispute were reportedly stoned and beaten. Four days later a force of some 100 police officers armed with *lathis* and guns attacked the village. Villagers were reportedly beaten indiscriminately and their property destroyed. According to policewoman constable, Neelkamal, who was visiting relatives in the village, "They just broke open the front door and rushed inside. My two sisters-in-law were beaten up and dragged outside by the police. When I told them I am also in the police, they just smirked and said 'so what, and started beating me up. They then dragged me outside and took me to the village school building where villagers were also rounded up. We were then taken to the police station. Here they started beating us once again and forcibly stripped our menfolk".

Twenty-nine women, five men and a 13-year-old boy were reportedly subjected to this treatment. Fourteen villagers were subsequently charged by the police with rioting and attempted murder. The incident provoked widespread protests throughout the state. On 5 September the Haryana chief minister announced a judicial inquiry. He acknowledged that police excesses had occurred, but denied allegations that village men had been forcibly stripped and paraded before the women. He announced the suspension of one police officer and the transfer of another.

Vulnerable Victims

Many Indians are members of the scheduled castes (castes which are recognized by the constitution as oppressed), or members of the scheduled tribes, known as *adivasis*. The term *dalit* -meaning "oppressed" - has been used to describe militant members of the scheduled castes. It has now gained broader currency and Amnesty International uses it in its broadest sense to describe all members of the scheduled castes, not merely the most militant.

Dalits and *adivasis* are the poorest and most vulnerable groups of people in India. Their special vulnerability has been recognized as requiring extra protection, notably in the Indian Constitution, Article 17 of which forbids untouchability and its practice in any form, and in the 1955 Untouchability offences Act (which was retitled the Civil Rights Protection Act in 1976). The Scheduled Castes and the Scheduled Tribes (Prevention of Atrocities) Act was passed in September 1989, making illegal some 24 social and economic abuses of the scheduled groups. The Act makes it a criminal offence for legal and administrative proceedings to be deliberately abused by police or security forces in case involving members of scheduled groups. It allows states to establish special courts to try such cases and provides for legal aid and for compensation for victims of abuse. Since this legislation was passed, however, human rights violations against *dalits* and *adivasis* have persisted, and police are frequently reported culpable.

In May 1990 the then Prime Minister, V.P. Singh, stated in parliament that his government would take the "sternest action" against those involved in violations against members of the scheduled groups. However, this and similar official statements have not resulted in an appreciable increase in the judicial investigation and prosecution of police officers involved in such offences. Not one special court was known to have been established under the Act by October 1991. In June 1990 a public outcry forced the Maharashtra state government to suspend several police officers and order a police inquiry into the killing of a teenage nomadic tribal youth and the torture of his pregnant sister.

The boy, Namdeo Atak, was reportedly beaten to death for trying to prevent seven police officers abducting and raping his sister, Parvati Rusankote. According to Parvati Rusankote, "They were all drunk and were dressed in ordinary clothes. They order a me to come with them. I refused. Then they began abusing me and two of them lifted me by my hands and feet". When Namdeo Atak insisted on accompanying his sister, he was also thrown into their jeep. Both were taken to the Thlzapur police station. Here, according to Parvati Rusankote: "Some of the seven policemen tied Namdeo to a table and began whipping him with their belts and hitting him with their *lathis.* Meanwhile, the rest caught hold of me. One of them gripped my hair and ripped apart my blouse, while another disrobed me and stood on my thighs.... They kept abusing me and also kicked me on the stomach".

Namdeo Atak was beaten unconscious. He and his sister were then taken back to their home where Namdeo Atak was beaten again in front of his father. Parvati Rusankote says that her brother died after four hours of beating: "The policemen left only when they were certain he was dead". A medical examination of Namdeo Atak's body reportedly found some 40 external injuries and many broken bones. However, the Maharashtra chief minister rejected calls for a judicial inquiry into the case.

Women are singled out for special protection under the Scheduled Castes and Scheduled Tribes Act; sexual assault of the women of the scheduled groups is an offence, as is their sexual exploitation by people in a "dominant position". However, police rape of *dalit* and *adivasi* women continues to be widely reported. In August 1991 the Bihar state government announced an inquiry, headed by a senior female police officer, into allegations that police had raped villagers in Chaksoagpur, Muzaffarpur district, in July. *Dalits* and *adivasis* are frequently tortured for political reasons, to deter them or punish them for involvement in organized resistance to economic exploitation. Often *adivasi* and *dalit* villages have been raided, and their inhabitants tortured and raped, by police acting in collusion with local ruling groups, such as landowners. Such abuses are common in Bihar, where most torture victims are landless labourers and their families campaigning for land reform and minimum wages. Landlords have often resorted to violence to suppress such campaigns with the assistance of criminal gangs or private armies, whose growth is believed to have been encouraged by the police since the late 1970s. In a number of cases local police officers are alleged to have cooperated with such groups or even participated in attacks on landless people.

Further, in May 1988, 23 women from Majhua village, Purnea District, were raped by police during a raid on the village, reportedly instigated by a local contractor as part of an attempt to intimidate villagers who had refused to work for less than the minimum wage. The police were armed and reportedly responded to any resistance with violence. The rape victims were said to include an 80-year-old woman, and a baby girl, aged one, was reportedly molested. The police are said to have maintained a 24-hour guard on the village to prevent publicity about the incident and a journalist who tried to publish a report on the incident in a local newspaper was threatened with death.

The district magistrate, said by some to be a friend of the contractor allegedly involved, denied the rapes had occurred and dismissed the allegations as fabricated by "criminal elements" in Majhua. When women from the village assembled to protest in Purnea, they were dispersed by the police with lathis. Forty million *adivasis*, 85 percent of India's total tribal population, inhabit the resource rich lands that stretch across central India. Most of them live below the poverty line; their rate of literacy is one-third of the national average. Economic development in the region, including forestry, mining and hydro-electric projects has resulted in increasing numbers of tribal peoples losing their traditional homes and livelihoods. Many now seek a living as small farmers, or as agricultural labourers working for large landowners, while others migrate to the cities in search of work.

In recent years tribal protests have centred on the questions of compensation for land lost to their communities, the distribution of surplus land, low wages, and autonomy for tribal regions. These demands have been supported by left-wing political groups, some of which - such as the Maoist revolutionaries known as *Naxalites* - have engaged in violent opposition to the authorities, particularly in Andhra Pradesh, Madhya Pradesh and Maharashtra. In an effort to crush such opposition, police have carried out widespread arrests and torture of adivasis suspected of involvement in such protests.

The *Naxalites* became active in the Bastar district of Madhya Pradesh, where the majority of the population are tribal peoples, in the early 1980s. In addition to organizing strikes and other forms of protest, the *Naxalites* carried out attacks on the police and murdered landowners and other civilians. In 1985 the state of Madhya Pradesh was declared a "disturbed area" under the Terrorist and Disruptive Activities (Prevention) Act (TADA). The strength of the civil police force in Bastar has been doubled in the past decade and several companies of armed police attached to the Madhya Pradesh Special Armed Force (SAF) are deployed in the district.

In July 1989 the PUCL issued a report on the situation in Bastar The PUCL had investigated the pattern behind an estimated 90 armed police raids on *adivasi* villages since the imposition of the TADA. The report stated: "A large contingent of armed police sometimes as many as 100 descend on a village.... They conduct indiscriminate beatings.... This May [19891 the police took three youths and buried them neck deep in the fields. After such violence the people, especially men, are taken to a police station. There the civil police take over.... They may hang the adivasis upside-down from the ceiling, or subject them to the infamous roller treatment and beat them up for days together".

The PUCL concluded: "many people suggest that the adivasis are being punished for giving food and shelter to the *Naxalites*. The ostensible purpose of the more sustained interrogations is to find the whereabouts of [the *Naxalites*]. The practice of using abominable third degree methods to extract information from the suspects is perhaps fairly common in most of the police stations of the country. But in Bastar it has absolutely no point since most policemen do not understand the language of the *adivasis* whom they torture".

In June 1991 the PUDR published a report of its investigation of police behaviour in the tribal village of Hadmatiya in Udaipur district, Rajasthan. In March 1990, according to this report, a local large landowner had lodged a complaint of trespass and theft against 37 villagers after they attempted to grow crop.; in a tank-bed to which they held traditional rights. The complaint was investigated by 11 police officers who visited the village on 5 March and reportedly provoked a riot by mistreating *adivasi* women. Several police officers were beaten. The police withdrew and filed charges of assault and attempted murder against the villagers. Some four weeks later, they also took direct reprisals, According to the PUDR, 14 jeeps, four trucks and a bus load of police officers, accompanied by some of the landowner's agents, surrounded the village and herded the villagers into a field. They then opened fire on the villagers, injuring 35. The women were stripped and beaten. The PUDR concluded that the purpose was to intimidate and terrorize the villagers for opposing the exploitative practices of landowners.

Torture during Counter-Insurgency

Torture is common in those areas where there are political

groups actively seeking independence or increased autonomy, especially when such demands are made by armed opposition groups. These groups are active particularly in Jammu and Kashmir, Punjab and the northeast states. In these areas, armed opponents of the government have been responsible for numerous human rights abuses, including torture, killing and hostage-taking, acts which Amnesty International condemns.

In these areas of armed opposition the security forces are empowered under the Terrorist and Disruptive Activities (Prevention) Act (TADA) to arrest suspects and detain them for up to one year without charge or trial for investigation into broadly defined offences. Detainees held under the TADA are usually denied bail. They must be tried in *camera*. During the trial the identity of witnesses can be kept secret and the accused is presumed guilty in four situations specified in the TADA.

Jammu and Kashmir : A Case Study

"I yesterday discharged a patient, aged 18-20, who had been in this hospital for three months. Twenty per cent or more of his body had suffered deep burns from a hot clothes-iron. These burns were... so serious that I and other doctors had only just succeeded in saving his life.... He had also been shot by a bullet in the armpit. His torturing with the clothes-iron had all been done during interrogation by the regular army at Sopor"

This statement from a doctor interviewed in a Srinagar hospital in December 1990 is typical of numerous reports of torture received from Jammu and Kashmir since late 1989, when the security forces were given increased powers following mounting violence in the state by armed opposition groups. More recently, Manzoor Ahmed Naikoo, a shopkeeper filmed in his hospital bed, accused the army of torturing him, telling his interviewer: "After tying me down, they removed my pyjamas. They tied some cloth round my penis and set it on fire.... Then they laid me face down, one man stood on my back. Another brought a rod and inserted it deep through my rectum. He kept thrusting it forward and back". Muzzaffar Shah told a similar story.

He also had ruptured intestines, liver and lungs. In the same film, made by the Indian video company, *Eyewitness,* army commander Lieutenant General S. Nath denied their allegations- "There is no torture. We have given very strict orders to our interrogators that they will not use any third degree methods". In November 1991 the government banned the film, citing "military security reasons". Control over the territory of Kashmir, two-thirds of which constitutes the Indian state of Jammu and Kashmir, has been disputed between India and Pakistan since 1947, leading twice to war between the two countries. Jammu and Kashmir is the only Indian state in which Muslims constitute a majority of the population.

The activities of armed Muslim militants seeking the state's independence from India have spread in recent years. Militant armed groups in the state have increasingly resorted to violence and extortion, and have taken, and sometimes killed, hostages. As a result, thousands of Hindus have fled the valley and live in camps in Jammu, the southern part of the state.

In response to this violence, Jammu and Kashmir was placed under President's Rule in July *1990.* The Armed Forces Special Powers Act, which provides the security forces with immunity from prosecution was imposed a month later. Since then, Indian security forces have been engaged in a major counter-insurgency operation against armed secessionist and fundamentalist groups and reports of torture and deaths in custody have increased dramatically.

Widespread human rights violations in the state since January 1990 have been attributed to the Indian army, and the paramilitary Border Security Force (BSF) and Central Reserve Police Force (CRPF). A 145,000- strong force of the CRPF was flown into the state at that time. Cordon-and-search operations are frequently conducted in areas of armed opposition activity or after attacks on the security forces, with districts being sealed off and house to-house searches conducted. Torture is reported to be routinely used during these combing operations as well as in army camps, interrogation centres, police stations and prisons. Indiscriminate beatings are common and rape in particular appears to be routine.

It is impossible to gauge the true extent of torture in Jammu and Kashmir. In July *1991* unofficial sources estimated that 15,000 people were being detained without trial in the state. Many of those detained since late *1989* have alleged after release that they were tortured or ill-treated in custody.

In November *1991* Dr. Kazi Massrat, the chief casualty officer at the Medical College Hospital, Srinagar, told a British journalist: "I must have treated 250 torture victims in the last year". He said they included men who had been forced to drink large quantities of fluid after having their penises tied tightly. Earlier, in June *1990,* recently released villagers from the community of Haihama-'Payerpora, Kupwara District, told another British journalist how they had been tortured while detained by the Indian army. When interviewed they still bore massive bruises, bums from electrodes and heated rods, cuts and rope sores. "One man, whose feet were bandaged up to the ankles, said a bed of coal had been covered with corrugated iron and a deep layer of sand, which slowed their progress when the prisoners were forced to run across it..." All had been released without charge after soldiers reportedly threatened to detain and torture them again if they should support the armed opposition.

Detailed information about torture and the victims is hard to obtain. Access to interrogation and detention centres run by the security forces is restricted even for lawyers. Most torture testimonies come from villagers tortured during, counter-insurgency raids, or from former detainees. The Srinagar bench of the Jammu and Kashmir High Court has been inundated with habeas corpus petitions of behalf of detainees at risk of torture - 3,000 petitions, according to the court's former Chief justice in an interview in December 1990, most of which had not been heard.

Information is made even harder to obtain by the strict control the security forces exercise over freedom of movement and freedom of expression. Victims are known to have written to Amnesty international, but none of their letters have reached the organization. Curfews are in force for long periods throughout the area, road blocks and check points policed by the security forces control all movement. Press censorship has been sporadically imposed. Some local newspapers have been banned and their offices sealed. International human rights organizations are also barred. Nevertheless, lawyers, civil liberties groups, and journalists have documented a consistent pattern of torture.

In Jammu and Kashmir, rape is practised, as part of a systematic attempt to humiliate and intimidate the local population during counter-insurgency operations. In May 1990 Mubina Gani, a teenage bride, was detained at a roadblock and raped by BSF soldiers on her way from the marriage ceremony to her husband's home. Her aunt, who was seven months pregnant, was also raped. The official explanation was that the wedding party had been caught in crossfire between two paramilitary units. The victims said that soldiers had fired on them without warning at the roadblock, killing one man and wounding several others before, raping the two women. Mubina Gani told one reporter: "We were crying bitterly. I told them I had not yet seen my husband. But they didn't listen.... Four to six persons raped me, I think".

This incident, when it was reported, captured the attention of both the Indian and international press. As a result an inquiry was instigated by the police, and a report from one senior police officer confirmed that the rapes had occurred. However, those responsible have not been brought to justice.

International publicity may also have been the reason 'why, in June 1991, the army invited a team from the Press Council of India to visit Kunan Poshpora, a village in the district of Kupwara, close to the Line of Control Which separates Indian-held Kashmir from Pakistan. Three months earlier, over 20 women had reportedly been raped when soldiers raided the village. The youngest victim was a girl of 13 named Misra, the oldest victim, named Jana, was aged 80.

Kunan Poshpora was raided on the night of 23-24 February 1991 during counter-insurgency operations by soldiers of the 4th Rajput Rifles. Local residents allege that several hundred soldiers arrived at the village at about 11 pm, cordoned it off and began house-to-house searches. Many men from the village were taken away an interrogated, in some cases under torture, about the activities of armed opposition groups. At the same time at least 23 women were reportedly raped in their homes at gunpoint. Some are said to have been gang-raped, others to have been raped in front of their children.

The incident was investigated by several different officials. A district magistrate, shocked by the allegations, concluded that there was sufficient evidence to warrant a full inquiry. The army strenuously denied the allegations of rape and torture and appointed an army brigadier to conduct an inquiry. He dismissed the allegations of rape as "malicious and untrue". On 18 March the divisional commissioner visited Kunan Poshpora: he reportedly recommended that a judicial inquiry be established to investigate the incident. A two-member team from the Press Council of India visited Kunan Poshpora for one day, following which it dismissed the statements of at least nine alleged rape victims because of what it described as inconsistencies. Medical evidence, which may have indicated rape, was described as "worthless".

The Indian Government has invoked the results of these inquiries in justification of its claim that rape did not occur. However, the government has withheld the medical findings on the Kunan Poshpura victims included in the Press Council's report and the findings of the inquiry conducted by the divisional commissioner have not been published. His reported recommendation that there should be a thorough investigation is not known to have been implemented.

Lawyers, journalists and others who have attempted to address human rights violations have been detained and tortured or ill-treated. Zahid Ali, a lawyer, was interrogated in the Gupkar Joint Interrogation Centre in Srinagar and reportedly forced under torture to confess to crimes he had not committed. He was apparently detained because of his work on behalf of political detainees. In June 1991 The Telegraph, Calcutta, reported that Noor Al Qamarain, a reporter for the *Kashmir Times,* had been detained for several days and questioned under torture about links between journalists and opposition groups.

People taken into custody for interrogation about armed opposition activities and those associated with such groups face more sustained torture than that meted out during counter-insurgency operations. The methods reported are brutal. In September 1991 a British journalist gave the following description of a torture victim he had seen in a Srinagar hospital. The victim was a villager from Chowki Bal, near the Line of Control, who had been detained and interrogated for three months by the BSF on suspicion of being a guerrilla. "A doctor lifted away [the] sheet gingerly, as though he were removing a huge bandage covering the body's length. Two scars ran parallel from his ribs to his groin. 'We sewed him up,' said [the doctor], who wished to remain unidentified. The Indian security forces burnt open his stomach with a clothes iron and then jumped on him with their boots.' [The victim) had lost 601b in the months in which his captors burned him, skewered him and applied electrodes to his penis."

The roller treatment - crushing bones with heavy rollers - is reported to be a particularly agonizing torture. A detainee released after eight weeks' interrogation witnessed it inflicted on a boy: "... a big long wooden log was rolled over his body from neck to foot by five men pushing down on it with all their strength. They broke bones and knees and crushed joints. The screams were terrible".

Although the government has announced inquiries, criminal charges and, in some cases, courts martial, Amnesty International knows of only two cases in which members of the paramilitary forces have been charged with offences constituting human rights violations. In the majority of cases, official inquiries have been conducted by the security forces themselves. Where the outcome is known, these inquiries have generally exonerated the security force personnel implicated. The minister of home affairs said in November 1991 that 50 members of the security forces had been suspended, and some imprisoned for human rights violations.

However, Amnesty International knows of no cases in which members of the security forces have been convicted of torturing prisoners.

Assam and the Northeast States: A Case Study

More than 220 hill tribes live in seven states in northeast India: Assam, Nagaland, Manipur, Arunachal Pradesh, Meghalaya, Mizoram and Tripura. They are ethnically, economically and socially different from inhabitants of other parts of India, from which the northeast is nearly cut off by Bangladesh.

Accusing the central government of neglect and exploitation, several tribal organizations in the northeastern states have advocated autonomy or independence and some have taken up arms in pursuit of these aims. Members of the security forces were first posted to the northeast Indian states in the 1950s. Widespread human rights violations have been attributed to the army, particularly the Assam Rifles, who report directly to the central government's Home and Defence Ministries and, to a lesser extent, to paramilitary forces and the police.

The most serious abuses have been reported from the areas where armed groups such as the National Socialist Council of Nagaland (NSCN), the People's Liberation Army of Manipur, the United Liberation Front of Manipur, and the United Liberation Front of Assam (ULFA), are active. The latter, notably, have captured and even killed hostages. All these organizations are banned. Torture and ill-treatment' occur routinely during counter-insurgency operations to flush out suspected members and supporters of these groups.

President's Rule was imposed in Assam on 28 November 1990, in response to a rising level of political violence. The state was declared a "disturbed area" and responsibility for maintaining order was given to the army. The ULFA was banned and a- major counter-insurgency offensive - "Operation Bajrang" - was launched. During this campaign, widespread human rights violations were reported. In January 1991 the *Times of India* reported: "Every single day reports pour in from different parts of the state about army atrocities, including killings, torture, rape and harassment.... The local newspapers are full of heart-rending reports of ordinary people being picked up by the army for no reason, women being raped and houses raided at uncanny hours".

Women and girls continue to be raped. On 6 October 1991 Raju Bartiah, a girl from Sutargaon, was raped by four soldiers and her body thrown into a pond. Her sisters identified the soldiers allegedly responsible and the inquest report confirmed signs of rape. Her family was granted Rs. 100,000 compensation but it is not known if the soldiers were brought to justice.

Between 28 November and 10 April 1991, when it suspended counter-insurgency operations, the army reportedly arrested 1,846 people in their search for ULFA militants. A further 1,000 were reportedly arrested by the police. Many were detained at random during mass raids on their villages; others were arrested at the army check posts or because they had broken curfew. They included peasants, labourers, academics, political and social activists, doctors, and businessmen. Youths and students were a particular target. Many of those arrested are believed to have been tortured. In December 1990, the army denied allegations of torture and rape during "Operation Bajrang", and claimed they were fabricated by political leaders with vested interests."

Over 100 *habeas* corpus petitions were filed in the Guwahati High Court between 27 November 1990 and March 1991 on behalf of people illegally detained and tortured during army operations in Assam. The High Court has upheld many petitions and ordered that the detainees be brought before it. Two brothers, Rituraj and Padmaraj Barua, who were detained by the army on 1 and 2 December 1990, both claimed they had been severely tortured for 20 days when the army produced them on the order of the court. The court ordered-that they be taken to the Guwahati Medical College hospital for treatment, and transferred them to judicial, custody. It awarded the brothers compensation for the torture they had suffered and eventually, on 4 April, released them on bail. However, the security forces have defied some High Court rulings.

In January 1991 the Guwahati High Court acquitted student Rajumoni Bezbarooah and ordered that he not be taken into custody without the permission of the university hostel warden. Rajumoni Bezbarooah was detained again some two months later and reportedly severely tortured at an army camp at Golaghat. He alleged that soldiers had destroyed the court's order when he showed it to them. Civil liberties organizations have played an important role in documenting human rights violations in Assam. In February, 1991 a team from the CPDR visited six districts in Assam. They gathered information on 49 cases of torture, 13 of rape, eight extrajudicial executions and one "disappearance". The PUDR also published a report on Assam, in May 1991. It concluded: "Most of the persons detained by the army were tortured.... We have interviewed many torture victims, visited three hospitals, met concerned doctors and gone through a number of court documents.

"Beating, stripping and hanging them upside down

and then beating on head and chest, thumping on chests with boots, pouring ice cold water, burying them up to chest and then beating or keeping a bucket over the head, squeezing testicles with clamps, dipping in cold water drums, forcefully keeping them awake for days together, denial of food or water are some of the forms of torture used. But the most common form is electric shocks. Sensitive parts of the body including ears, tongue, armpits, genitals and head were repeatedly given electric shocks sometimes in progressively higher voltages. With electrodes at each temple the brain was subjected to electric waves."

An earlier campaign for tribal autonomy in Assam was launched in March 1987 by a tribal association, the All-Bodo Students' Union (ABSU). The campaign began with strikes and demonstrations but increasingly involved bombings, arson attacks and killings of targeted individuals. The Assam Armed Police were sent into Bodo-inhabited areas of the state with orders to deal firmly with the campaign, and Bodo districts were placed under the TADA.

There have since been numerous reports of the torture and killing of Bodo civilians and hundreds have been arbitrarily detained. Amnesty International has details of the alleged torture of 80 Bodos arrested between February 1988 and November 1989. The youngest was an illiterate 12-year-old boy arrested during a raid on his village, Lailang Para, in Darrang district, in September 1989. The methods of torture described range from beatings and asphyxiation to being crushed with heavy rollers and subjected to mock execution.

Rape and ill-treatment of Bodo women by the police and the security forces have also been widely reported. Rape often occurs during raids on villages in search of tribal militants. In March 1989,15 tribal girls were reportedly raped at Rupnathpur, Kokrajhar district, by members of the Assam

Police Task Force (APTF) who had raided the village. At the end of June two Bodo girls, 10-year-old Binati Nable and Aswani Brahan, aged 15, of Goyvari village in Kokrajhar district were gang-raped by police officers during a raid. Both girls were examined the same day by a doctor at Banargeon, who said he was not authorised to give a report. At the instigation of the All Assam Tribal Women Welfare Association a complained the next day with the local police superintendent. An examination of the two girls at Kokrajhar hospital confirmed that they had been subjected to sexual intercourse. The police were informed but no action appears to have been taken.

In Manipur state, hundreds of villagers in and around Oinam were detained and tortured in July 1987 during "Operation Bluebird, ostensibly conducted to search for NSCN members who had earlier attacked a military outpost. Over 300 villagers were interrogated and beaten - some of them so severely that their limbs were broken - given electric shocks, burned with cigarettes or hung upside-down. Pregnant women were beaten and some had miscarriages as a result. Some villagers had chili powder inserted into sensitive parts of their bodies. Others were buried up to their necks and led to believe they would be killed. The youngest victim was one year old, the oldest a man of 65. Thirty-four were children aged 12 and under. Boys of 15 and 16 were tortured with electric shocks.

Local civil liberties lawyers worked hard to ensure that the victims received redress. On 6 June 1988 the Guwahati High Court directed the Imphal Sessions Court to record first-hand evidence from the villagers about the incident. The sessions court concluded its hearings on 21 April 1990. The case is now pending before the Guwahati High Court. Throughout the hearings the security forces have repeatedly attempted to intimidate witnesses and their relatives through illegal detention, torture and death threats. Some of the villagers were arrested by the Assam Rifles and tortured to make them retract their evidence. Others were arrested after they had testified in court. The UN Special Rapporteur on torture, asking the Indian Government about this, was told that these reports were false and politically motivated.

The victims are not only waiting for redress some four years later, but many reportedly still suffer from the effects of torture. The Naga Doctors' Forum and the Drug Action Forum of West Bengal examined 104 of the villagers. According to their August 1990 report, all but three of the villagers were found to be mentally unwell and many still suffered pain and disability from injuries inflicted by torture. Despite the gravity of this incident and the detailea allegations of human rights violations, some of which were confirmed in court, the central government refused to 'Order an independent investigation into the allegations. Only a local police inquiry was held, which confirmed some torture allegations.

Of the armed struggles for local autonomy in northeast India, the Naga insurgency is the oldest. Since 1947 the 1.2 million people of Nagaland have been policed by some 150,000 Indian troops. In October 1990 troops unleashed what one newspaper, *The Hill* Express, described as "a reign of terror" after NSCN guerrillas ambushed an army patrol near Botsa, killing three soldiers and injuring several others. In an apparent attempt to root out NSCN members, the Assam Rifles conducted raids on several villages. According to press reports, villagers were beaten with fists, sticks and rifle butts and tortured by having chilli powder rubbed in their eyes and water forced up their nostrils. The victims included a man of 65 who was paralysed and Shri Neo, a villager who had been deaf and mute since birth. Both were reportedly beaten because they were unable to answer soldiers' questions. Over 30 people required hospital treatment for injuries suffered during these raids.

Amnesty International has received affidavits sworn by 16 of the victims. Shri Keveikuolie, a 28-year-old man from Narhema village, gave the following description of his treatment: "Two slapped me while the third held me by my hair. As soon as I fell down, five to six started kicking and hitting me with their rifle butts and barrels all over my body. They then took me to the side of the road and propped me against the wall. I could not stand and I fell down. They then put the barrel of a rifle inside my mouth and asked me either to speak or die".

Rape by the security forces is one of the most frequently reported human rights violations in Tripura state, where the Tripura National Liberation Front (later renamed the Tribal National Front) has resorted to killings and kidnapping in pursuit of its demand for increased rights for Tripura's tribal population. In April 1989 opposition members of the state assembly alleged that there had been 100 cases of rape by the security forces in the previous few months.

Rape usually occurs during counter-insurgency operations and gang-rapes of tribal women by members of the police force and soldiers are frequently reported. In June 1988 the Assam Rifles conducted a cordon-and- search operation in Ujan Maidan, Khowai district, in pursuit of members of the outlawed Tripura National Volunteers. At least 14 tribal women said they were raped during the search and were admitted to Khowai government hospital, one woman said that her husband had been tied tip. The youngest victim was 12 years old. The state government dismissed the allegations but admitted that some women might have been beaten. An inquiry conducted by the police and Assam Rifles found that one woman had "probably" been raped and that two other's could have been molested, but no independent investigation was conducted.

In June 1991,14 tribal women from Gachipara village in Tripura's Dharma Nagar district were dragged from their huts and raped by police officers, while the men were herded into a corner of the village.

As of now 2010 human rights violation cases of police and armed forces are ever increasing in India. Distrubed areas are more prone to this. Delhi police is also notorious in such matters. Many cases of false implication of innocent persons, custodial deaths surface in media very frequently.

4

Impunity: Condoning Custodial Violence

> "The truest help we can render an afflicted man is not to take his burden from him, but to call out his best energy, that he may be able to bear the burden."
>
> —*Phillips Brooks*

It is pertinent to note that successive Indian governments have consistently failed to ensure that proper investigations — a prerequisite for bringing the perpetrators to justice or obtaining compensation for the victims - are held in cases of custodial violence. As the Indian press has frequently observed, investigations often appear to be intended more as a response to public pressure than as a systematic means of addressing and preventing human rights violations. The result is that very few police are ever brought to justice for torture.

Article 21 of the Constitution lays down that nobody may be deprived of his life or liberty except by a process established by law. Sections 330 and 331 of the Indian Penal Code say that torture of an individual to extract information is a crime punishable with up to 10 year's of imprisonment.

Death due to torture is murder as defined in Sections

302 IPC for which the maximum punishment is death. Therefore the only lawful course for the Government in the event of death in police custody is to arrest the official concerned and to prosecute him under the above sections. This has not been done in any instance in the country. Normally, a police officer is merely transferred or suspended.

> ".... the Government has done pretty little to arraign the guilty. Its reaction depends on the reaction of the people and the press. If the death has not attracted much attention, it is ignored. If it has drawn the attention of the Opposition and the press, a magisterial inquiry is ordered. If the death provokes-public reaction in a big way, a judicial inquiry is ordered. And yet, no inquiry makes any difference to the victims family. Nor does it restrain the police from repeating the act".

International human rights standards require that governments undertake full investigations into all reports of torture and deaths in custody and bring those responsible to justice. Failure to do so means that the victims and their relatives are denied justice and that the truth is withheld from society at large. Most importantly, the failure to identify and bring' those responsible to justice sends a clear message to the perpetrators that their actions are condoned and may effectively encourage them to commit further torture. In India, there is a substantive body of evidence that governments and official agencies have made special efforts to cover-up human rights violations and prevent the Police and security forces from being punished. Amnesty International knows of only three out of 415 cases of custodial deaths which occurred since 1985 in which police officers accused of torturing people to death have been convicted by the courts. The only states in which this is known to have happened are Andhra Pradesh, Karnataka (one out of six cases), and Orissa (one out of six cases). In August 1988 two police officers were sentenced to five and eight years' imprisonment on charges of culpable homicide not amounting to murder for assault causing the death in detention of Kashinath Nayak on 3 May 1985 in Orissa. In November 1990, after protracted legal proceedings, seven police officials were sentenced to various terms of imprisonment, including two life sentences for murdering lawyer M.A. Rasheed, whose body was found two days after he had been taken away by Karnataka police officers. The state's home minister at the time, who had subsequently resigned over the incident and who was accused of instigating his murder, was acquitted.

The most recent case known to Amnesty International resulted in a Gujarat High Court judgment on 23 October 1991; six police officers were sentenced to six years imprisonment for beating Kantuji Mohansinh to death in 1982 and destroying the evident of their offence. The same police officers had previously been acquitted in May 1983 but, in the only such case known to Amnety International, the state appealed against that judgment to the court which set aside the acquittal and convicted the police officers. Police officers have been prosecuted in cases in other states but, to Amnesty Internationals knowledge, none of these cases resulted in convictions. In Manipur. Rajasthan and Jammu and Kashmir no prosecutions or convictions whatsoever are known to have occurred. Amnesty International's data may-be incomplete because not all prosecutions are necessarily reported.

However, a study by the PUDR published in August 1991 in New Delhi found evidence of a similar pattern: only nine out of 58 cases of death in custody in Delhi between 1980 and 1991 had resulted in criminal prosecutions. The PUDR concluded that a lack of "demonstrative follow-up action against the erring policemen" was the primary reason for the rise in custodial deaths.

The very few prosecutions that have occurred have almost invariably been the result of years of determined struggle by relatives of the victims seeking justice, rather than official initiatives to enforce the law. Only rarely have relatives succeeded in initiating criminal prosecutions of police officers allegedly responsible for torture.

Amnesty International believes that it is often direct or indirect pressure from the executive arm of government which prevents prosecutions. In Uttar Pradesh impunity was effectively granted to members of the Provincial Armed Constabulary (PAC) and prison officials who had allegedly tortured and killed Muslims in their custody during communal rioting in Meerut in May 1987. Hundreds of Muslims were seen being taken away by the PAC; dozens never returned. They are believed to have been secretly killed and their bodies thrown into nearby canals.

Two judicial investigations were instituted by the Uttar Pradesh state government: one by Justice Srivastava; the other by former auditor general Gian Prakash. But the inquiry reports were never published. The state government refused to table them in the legislative assembly. According to one authoritative source, the Prakash report "confirmed that 40-60 youths were indeed taken from Hashimpura in PAC trucks and were since untraceable". One resident commented: "So many of our young men were killed... We know the killers, we see them every day. Even the authorities know them. But nothing has been done and nothing will be."

Some of those arrested by the PAC were taken to prison. Seven of them died in Fatehgarh jail of injuries received in police stations and the jail. A magisterial inquiry was held as a result of which two jail guards and two convict warders were suspended. Departmental proceedings were instituted against three prison officials and three cases of murder were registered. However, no prosecutions were initiated.

Suspension is the usual official response in the face of a public outcry when someone is killed in custody. In 70 of the cases of death in custody listed 146 police officers and other specials allegedly responsible were suspended. In many of these cases, suspension appears to have been simply a delaying tactic, until public pressure had subsided or the resources of the victims and their relatives had been exhausted. In August *1989*, when seven police were family suspended five years after Mohammed Idris had been tortured to death in Calcutta's Lal Bazar police station, *The* Statesman commented:

> "What is ... unfortunate is that it took such a prolonged inquiry to identify the culprits thereby suggesting that there was an attempt at suppression. And while an ordinary citizen would have faced a long prison term, if not the gallows, for such a crime, all that the police authorities have done so fair is to suspend the guilty. What incidents such as these demonstrate is not only the double standards that are followed in the application of the laws, last, also, the viciousness that has become an integral part of the police system."

Police officers suspended in connection with deaths in custody have sometimes been promoted shortly afterwards. The director general of police in Calcutta told the press on 11 August *1989* that the officer-in charge of the anti-burglary section, suspended the day before in connection with the death of Mohammed Idris, would be promoted as assistant commissioner if acquitted. After the death of navy seaman T.

Muralidharan a number of police officers were suspended, but all were subsequently reinstated and was of them were promoted. In early 1991 a police officer wanted for questioning in connection with the gang-rape of a tribal woman in Orissa was promoted on the express orders of the state police headquarters. Following the torture and death in police custody of Dwarika Thakur in September 1991 in Jehanabad district. Bihar, and the suspension of the two officers allegedly responsible, a press report commented:

> "But as numerous such cases in the past have shown, suspension is no way to punish police officials. In Bihar police officials are suspended one day to pacify the anger of the people against police excesses, and the suspension is revoked the next day. Very often, the officials, after getting their suspensions revoked, get a "reward" posting. Indeed in Bihar the number of times a policeman has been suspended, particularly on charges of torturing arrested persons, is taken as a symbol of his professional prowess".

Even if judicial inquiries identify the alleged culprits, state governments frequently fail to prosecute them. In October 1988 the *Deccan* Herald, a Bangalore newspaper, pointed to several cases in which the Andhra Pradesh state government had failed to take: "any action against men in uniform even when they have been held responsible for killing". The newspaper reminded its readers that three separate judicial inquiries into recent deaths in detention had concluded that police officers were directly responsible and had named the officers responsible for what in one case had been described as a "'cold-blooded murder". Despite the evidence produced by these inquiries the state government of Andhra Pradesh had initiated no action to punish the culprits: "This is not the first time cops have been found guilty of excesses. Yet, apart from nominal suspensions and perhaps a transfer or two, the culprits in uniform get away scot-free, despite promises by the Government to prosecute them".

There is compelling evidence that the police and other security forces feel free to act with impunity in violating the rights of those in their custody. In parts of the country in which armed opposition are active, immunity from prosecution is explicitly sanctioned by specific legislation. Elsewhere, members of the police and security forces are able to act with impunity because of an informal but nevertheless pervasive and well established system of official Complicity in covering up human rights violations.

Legally Sanctioned Impunity

Special laws in force in states where there is armed insurgency explicitly grant immunity from prosecution to the police and other security force personnel. The Armed Forces (Special Powers) Act, currently in force in Punjab, Jammu and Kashmir, and Assam and other northeast states, gives the security forces wide powers to make arrests, conduct searches without warrant, and to shoot to kill. Section 4 of the act states: "Any commissioned officer, noncommissioned officer or any other person of equivalent rank in the armed forces may... fire upon or otherwise use force, even to the causing of death, against any person who is acting in contravention of any law or order for the time being in force in the disturbed area prohibiting the assembly of five or more persons or the carrying of weapons or of things capable of being used as weapons..."

In exercising the powers provided in the act, the security forces are granted immunity in advance from possible prosecution. Ordinary legal safeguards do not apply. Section 6 of the act reads: "No prosecution, suit or other legal proceeding shall be instituted, except with the previous sanction of the Central Government, against any person in respect of anything done or purported to be done in the exercise of the powers conferred by this Act".

When the provisions of this act were scrutinized recently by the UN Human Rights Committee, established to monitor governments' adherence to the ICCPR, one member of the Committee drew particular attention to the manner in which such laws can facilitate human rights violations: "In this section which gives immunity both from prosecution and from civil process there is a very dangerous word ...*Purported is* the dangerous thing because anyone killing anybody can say 'Well I thought I was performing my functions."

Amnesty International believes that these provisions of the Act have been interpreted by the security forces as a licence to torture and kill with impunity.

Ordinarily, torture is a crime under Indian law: Sections 330 and 331 of the Indian Penal Code (IPC) provide imprisonment for up to 10 years for anyone convicted of causing hurt to extort a confession or information about an offence. Section 302 makes murder liable to life imprisonment or Section 29 of the Police Act, 1861, makes a police officer who commits "any unwarrantable personal violence to any person in his custody" liable to loss of pay for three months or imprisonment not exceeding three months.

Public servants, however, including police and executive magistrates, enjoy considerable protection from prosecution: Section 197 of the Code of Criminal Procedure provides that they can not be prosecuted without prior permission from the government - either state or central government - which employs them. That protection was further strengthened with parliament's adoption of the Code of Criminal Procedure

(Amendment) Bill in September 1991. This protects all government officers from any prosecutions for actions taken in the course of duty when a state is under direct rule from the central government. In those states, officials may be prosecuted only with the central government's permission.

Non-legal Systems of Impunity

Several well-established procedural techniques for evading prosecution for human rights violations provide informal but effective impunity for police and security forces throughout the country. These include the systematic cover-up of human rights violations by the police, the security forces, and the government. These techniques are supported by institutional practices and official policies which provide minimal sanctions against those few police or soldiers who are held accountable for custodial violence.

The police regularly resort to a range of techniques to cover-up instances of custodial violence: failure to register complaints, acknowledge detention or to apply other legal safeguards; denial of responsibility; falsification of judicial records and post-mortem reports sometimes by having them carried out at police hospitals; intimidation of witnesses and complainants; and influencing police inquiries by having them conducted by police from the same branch and delaying their outcome and prosecutions.

It is not only the police who use these methods; they can often rely on the active complicity of medical doctors, executive magistrates and other officials who contribute to cover-ups by writing false reports or suppressing evidence of police torture. Police cover-ups are so common and frequent an occurrence that police officers have themselves acknowledged their existence: "Everybody knows that the police have their own methods to' maintain law and order but you surely don't expect anybody to admit to this officially", one police officer was quoted as telling a Sunday Daily reporter in late 1987.

Failure to Comply with Legal Requirements

Chapter 5 of the Code of Criminal Procedure (CrPC) lays down the rules the police have to follow when arresting and detaining people. These include informing detainees of the nature of their offence, the grounds for their arrest, and their entitlement to bail. The police are also obliged to produce detainees before a magistrate within 24 hours of arrest. All arrests have to be reported by the officer in charge of the police station to the district magistrate. Non-compliance with these and other provision for arrest and detention specified in law carry penalties of up to seven years imprisonment The police are obliged to register in writing and keep on record all information relating to the commission of an offence.

In some cases, the police have sought to evade responsibility for death in their custody by denying that the victims had been arrested or by refusing to register a complaint. This was acknowledged by the *Hindustan Times in* a February 1991 editorial: "'Many cases of atrocities still go unreported because of fear of reprisals from perpetrators of the crimes and refusal of the police to register such complaints". There is no way of knowing how many victims of human rights violations or their relatives have been frustrated in their attempts to bring their complaints before the authorities and to seek redress, but the evidence suggests that they are many.

Indeed, the National Police Commission (NPC) acknowledged the "malady of non-registration of complaints when crimes are reported at police stations", which it recognized as particularly prevalent when complaints related to misconduct by the police, and especially when those complaints were made by the poor. ''We are aware that a considerable number who are aggrieved on account of police inactivity or indifference belong to the weaker sections of society who do not have enough resources to pursue their complaints in higher quarters". The commission noted what it considered to be a tendency on the part of the police to suppress information about alleged misconduct, adding that this became marked' when the misconduct was said to have occurred during the discharge of their duties by the police The commission added "Examples are: allegations of torture when a person is being interrogated by police during investigation.."

The death of Narasimha Raju, a 20-year-old youth, in the Tilak Park police station in Tumkur, Karnataka, is one example of an attempted police cover-up which came unstuck. According to eye-witnesses, he was taken away by two police officers on 8 July 1990. The same evening a neighbour went to the police station and saw Narasimha Raju there. The young man appeared unwell; the neighbour was told by the police not to come again. The police had told Narasimha Raju's relatives that foe would be released after signing some papers in connection with a theft, but three days later he had still not appeared. They then went to the police station to inquire about him, only to be told by police sub-inspector that he had never been there. They applied to court the next day, arguing that he had been arrested illegally, and again encountered a police denial.

The truth as to what had occurred emerged only when Mutta a original suspect who was detained, at Tilak Park police station at the same time came forward. He stated that on 11 July Narasimha Raju had been taken to the police station's "crime room" and severely beaten by the police, and had died the next morning. He said that he personally had helped load Narasimha Raju's body into a police van, assisted by the van driver. The body was eventually discovered no less than 200 kilometres away, in Chikmagalur. A post-mortem examination noted several injuries on the body. Three police officers were subsequently charged with the illegal arrest, torture and murder of Narasimha Raju, and with destroying evidence. Amnesty International does not know whether they were brought to trial.

Sometimes, the police deliberately fail to record the arrest of persons detained for interrogation, although it is required by law. One such case occurred in West Bengal in October 1987 when two brothers were arrested. One of them, Manohar Jaiswal, died the following day, 24 October. The police said he was the victim of an assault by unknown miscreants, but his brother maintained he had been hung upside down and beaten with lathis by a constable and a sub-inspector of police. A subsequent inquiry by the deputy commissioner revealed that the two brothers had been arrested on 23 October, but that their names were not registered in the general diary or in the "lock-up register". It found also that Manoharjaiswal had been "assaulted severely" inside the police station. Five police officers were suspended as a result for "not maintaining any record of the youth's arrest and for being "morally responsible" for his death, but they are not known to have been prosecuted.

The police also frequently fail to bring detainees before a magistrate within 24 hours of arrest, as the law requires. One reason, clearly, is that this may expose the fact that a suspect has been tortured or ill-treated. In January 1990 Vijay Karan, then commissioner of the Delhi police, made an unannounced visit to Shriniwaspuri police station in South

Delhi where at least one death as a result of police torture is believed to have occurred. His Visit resulted in the release of nine men who were able to complain to the commissioner that they had been held for several days in connection with a murder investigation but had not been brought before a magistrate within 24 hours of arrest.

The NPC also pointed to police distorting the facts in First Information Reports (FIR). These are used to record the first complaint about an offence and, unlike statements recorded by the police during investigation, can be admitted in evidence during legal proceedings. The NPC commented: "The evidentiary importance attached to the First Information Report... has led to the malpractice of police officers delaying the recording of [a] First Information Report in its natural form and compiling it in a made up manner after taking advice from persons with experience in procedural law."

Several recent cases illustrate the sort of malpractice that has occurred. In one, the report of a the deputy superintendent of the Bombay police into the death in detention of a farmer, Ramu Aba Bhandirge, in November 1989, was described by two high court judges as "not only irregular but illegal". They noted that the FIR had not been filed and that the police inquiry - which had absolved the police by concluding that Ramu Aba Bhandirge had died a natural death - had taken on an "illegal colour". In fact, there were allegations that he had been beaten to death by the police. In another case, Involving a similarly auspicious death In custody. An Andhra Pradesh High Court judge found that the "records of the police station had been tampered with and superior officers were kept in the dark about the lock-up death". In West Bengal, the death of a 50-year-old robbery suspect, Matiar Rahman Gazi, in May 1989 was first said by the police to have resulted from his trying to "escape from a moving van". Another person arrested with him, however, refuted this and said that the dead man had been severely tortured after his arrest by being hanged upside down and beaten. A judicial magistrate who examined the case found that the police had tampered with the records: the initial police version attributing the death to an attempt to jump from a speeding police jeep had been "scored through and later rewritten" so as to suggest that Matiar Rahman Gazi had died when he had jumped from a terrace in a bid to evade arrest. "It is really shocking, disturbing and unthinkable to note that a portion of a judicial record had been tampered with in such a naked fashion", the magistrate commented.

Subsequently, the chief judicial magistrate for the area found that there was a prima *facie* case against the officer in charge of Hasnabad police station, where the death occurred. As in many other such cases, there were fears that the police would intimidate witnesses. The police officer was instructed not to enter the Hasnabad police station area as "he may gain influence over the witnesses, or threaten them and hamper the trial proceedings".

Distortion of Cause of Death

In a number of cases, the police have attempted to cover up the torture of detainees who died in their custody by providing false information about the circumstances of the deaths and by denying any responsibility for them. Sometimes they have announced that deaths were due to suicide or illness, accidents, assaults by others, or to injuries sustained when the prisoner tried to escape or resist arrest, Some deaths have been attributed to armed "encounters", with the police denying that the victims were in custody at the time of death.

Police accounts have sometimes been contradictory. The

death in detention of T. Muralidharan, a navy seaman who was found hanged at Vijayawada police station in Andhra Pradesh in September 1986, was said by the police to have occurred after he had collapsed in front of the police station and was taken to hospital. Subsequently, the police revised this and said that he had hanged himself at the police station while mentally unbalanced, after he had tried to throw himself into a canal. An injury on his wrist was said by the police to have been caused by a "rat-bite". A senior naval officer who investigated the case, however, found seven injuries on his body, and another man who had been held at Vijayawada police station said he had seen the seaman being brought into the police station and had heard "sounds of torture". This informant also claimed to have heard a voice say, "he is finished", and to have seen the dead man's body being put into a police jeep. A judicial inquiry later concluded that T. Muralidharan's death had resulted from police torture.

Deaths in custody are often attributed to suicide by the police. Chatragadda Sambaiah's death occurred in August 1988 at Eluru police station, Andhra Pradesh. He had been arrested for possessing stolen property. The police said he had hanged himself with a string that he wore around his waist as a belt. His wife alleged that police gave her Rs 2,000 and sent her family to her parents' village after threatening retaliation if she disclosed the circumstances of the death. According to a report in the *Deccan Herald*, in October 1988, the string used as a belt is normally silk or cotton, (and not strong enough to hang a grown man), but that which the police exhibited was a thick nylon rope.

Officials have also frequently claimed that particular deaths in custody were the results of illnesses such as epilepsy, tuberculosis or heart failure, even when the victims were young and apparently healthy. Although some deaths undoubtedly do result from natural causes it is also true that many have been wrongly attributed to natural causes in an attempt to conceal torture. Prakash Ramchandra Kamble, 22 years old and unemployed, died in the custody of Naupada police, Thane, in Maharashtra on 11 November 1987. He had been arrested on suspicion of stabbing someone. The police said he died of heart failure, but this was challenged by a friend who had been arrested at the same time. He said that Prakash Kamble had been brutally tortured by being forced to lie down on a table, with his hands and feet handcuffed, and beaten with a leather belt and iron rods in an attempt to make him confess.

An inquest conducted by the Thane executive magistrate reportedly found that the rear left part of the young man's skull had caved in. Both his ears were blackened with bruises, and one was swollen; his back and shoulders were bruised, blood had congealed on a wound on his left leg; his genitals were bruised, the skin on his right knee had peeled off and his left thigh was swollen. These injuries were believed to have been caused by a belt or sharp instrument. The post-mortem examination found that his death was due to shock caused by multiple injuries. In January 1988 hundreds of people marched to the Thane police station demanding that his killers be brought to justice. However, no action is known to have been taken.

In this case, as in many others the evidence of doctors has been important in challenging police assertions that detainees died due to illness. When Vemula. Venkatesh, a factory worker, died in custody in Andhra Pradesh in October 1988, the police said death was due to tuberculosis. But relatives of the dead man alleged that he had been tortured and a post-mortem examination reportedly revealed: "Multiple injuries, burn marks and injuries made by a blunt instrument on the abdomen". According to doctors, there was no evidence" to support the police claim that he had died of tuberculosis".

In some cases, relatives of deceased prisoners have been put under pressure by the police to sign false statements suggesting that the victims had died from diseases or illnesses from which they had never suffered. Bashir Ahmad died in detention in August 1991 after he was arrested by the police in Andhra Pradesh in connection with a theft. The police said he had died during a fit of epilepsy, but the APCLC, a state civil liberties group, learned that Bashir Ahmed's mother had apparently agreed to sign a statement prepared by the police, stating that her son suffered from epilepsy when this was untrue. The dead man's body reportedly bore scars and other injuries on the nose, neck, right shoulder, back, palms, knees and feet. One leg was badly torn. The injuries were probably inflicted by a blunt instrument and were highly suggestive of torture.

Sometimes the police have admitted that prisoners have died from beatings but said these were inflicted by people other than the police, or were administered by police officers acting in self-defence. Mahendra Singh, a 28-year-old man from the Chhoti Basti in Pushkar, Rajasthan, his 22-year-old brother, Kiran, and their 50-year-old father, Banne, died in police custody on 26 June 1988. The police said the three men had attacked police officers when they were searched for drugs and had been lynched by local residents, although no case was registered against those said to have carried out the lynching. Local residents, however, have contested this version and a man who had been held at the police station on the night of 25 June disclosed that the three men had been brought in by police officers who tied their hands and feet and beat them incessantly with lathis until they died. The three were taken to Ajmer hospital but were reported to be dead on arrival.

The deputy superintendent of police, Ajmer, who investigated the case found that the local police version had been "fabricated". A case of murder was brought by the criminal intelligence department and orders were given for the arrest of five police officers, who were said by the deputy inspector general of the CID to have been solely responsible for the deaths. A magisterial inquiry was ordered but its outcome is not known. All 18 police officers in Pushkar police station were transferred. Five were arrested and charged with murder, but no trial is known to have taken place. In states where armed opposition groups are active police, para- military forces and the army often allege that political suspects have died while trying to escape or in armed "encounter".

The exact circumstances of death in such cases can be particularly difficult to establish as police officers are the only witnesses. Their descriptions of what occurred are often so identical as to appear rehearsed. "Escaped" prisoners almost never return home nor are their bodies found. In the case of "encounter" deaths, witnesses sometimes have seen, the victims being arrested earlier or while they were in custody but the 'encounters" in which they are said to have died rarely result in the death of police officers and are invariably witnessed only by the police, raising suspicion that police claim there was an "encounter" in order to cover up deaths in custody resulting from torture or ill-treatment. In Manipur, during counter-insurgency operations in Oinam, at least 11 and possibly, as many as 15 men were deliberately killed by the Assam Rifles in July 1987. The Assam Rifles claimed that the dead were either killed in armed "encounters" between their soldiers and the NSCN or else had been shot while "trying to escape". This was disputed by eye-witnesses, and senior police officers investigating the alleged "encounters" were said to have found that "they wore nothing but 'cold blooded' shooting of villagers". The Guwahati High Court also rejected the explanation put forward; by the Assam Rifles when it ruled that the families of B. Wa and P. I. Ring, two of those killed, should receive compensation.

In May 1990 another death occurred in the custody of the Assam Rifles. S. Joel, a 17-year-old, was shot while "trying to escape", according to the police report. Two days before his death the boy had been taken by a patrol to the Assam Rifles' headquarters in Somsai, Ukhrul. The following day he was taken to his brother's house, already showing signs of torture which caused him to have difficulty in walking. He was apparently beaten by soldiers in front of his relatives, who feared for his life, and then taken back to the Somsai headquarters and tortured with electric shocks. The next day, 25 May, his dead body was taken to Ukhrul Police Station. The Assam Rifles attributed his death to has attempting to escape, a claim which, in view of his seriously weakened physical condition, appears highly incredible.

Killings of prisoners in Punjab have also been attributed falsely 55 to armed "'encounters" or to escape attempts

Intimidation of Witnesses

Police often interfere with evidence by intimidating witnesses. Several Judicial officials have confirmed this practice. Justice S.C. Deb of the Calcutta High Court, appointed to inquire into the death of Mohammed Idris in the custody of the Calcutta police, reported in relation to that case:

> "A show of investigation was made by some officers. Many alleged outsiders and policemen and officers were

> tutored to make untrue statements and their tutored statements were recorded ... An untrue report was intentionally made thereafter by the then Assistant Commissioner of Police (G) Enforcement Branch, Calcutta, to mislead our Hon'ble Chief Minister.

A judge investigating the April 1985 death in Andhra Pradesh of Angadi Prabhakara Rao also pointed to this practice: "before ordering a judicial inquiry, the minimum that is expected is the transfer of the concerned police officers so that witnesses may come forward and depose against the police free from fear".

In some cases the police have gone to extraordinary lengths to prevent the truth emerging, including the confiscation and disposal of bodies of alleged torture victims to prevent their exhumation. This occurred in the case of Basudev Ravani, a 55 year-old coal miner in Bihar's Dhanbad district, arrested in July 1989. "The police said he died of alcohol poisoning and a post-mortem examination at the Loyabad Central Hospital was apparently conducted under police guard, The police then buried the body at the cemetery at Telipan. Only then were the dead man's family informed of his death. However, the police apparently refused to say what they had done with his body.

Consequently, the relatives went to the hospital, where they were told that the police had found an "unidentified" body and heard that it had been buried at the Telipaia cemetery. They went there at once to exhume it, suspecting that Basudev Ravani might have been tortured or beaten to death. When they arrived at- the cemetery, 10 or 12 police officers from the Loyabad police station also appeared; they apparently abused the relatives., poured kerosene over the exhumed body and set light to it. Subsequently, a magisterial inquiry questioned the police version of the detainee's death and the officer in charge of the Loyabad police station was suspended. It is not known, however, whether any police officers were prosecuted in relation to Basudev Ravani's death.

More recently, the Punjab police tried to frustrate attempts by relatives to obtain a second post-mortem report to establish the cause of death of Manjit Singh, himself a police constable, who had been arrested on 8 August 1991 on suspicion of murder. He was admitted to hospital nine days later and had died there. The police said that he was suffering from dysentery, but he apparently made a dying declaration to hospital doctors that he had been tortured' by his former Chandigarh police colleagues. An Inquest was ordered and a medical report was made but the contents were not disclosed. However, there was speculation in the press that the post-mortem report had corroborated the torture allegations and noted contusions on the left side of the body, between the knees and groin, above the ankles and on the face.

After the post-mortem examination, Manjit Singh's father said the police had tried to force him to sign a paper, but that he had refused. If he had signed the paper the police would have been able to claim the body for cremation, despite an order issued to them by a judicial magistrate to stay the cremation until 19 August so as to allow the family the opportunity to have a second autopsy conducted by a board of doctors at the Post Graduate Institute.

In several other cases, relatives of victims of custodial deaths have said the police tried to bribe them, offering them money to keep quiet. The father-in-law of Narasimha Rao, for example, reportedly said police officers had visited him and "promised to pay him a large sum of money if he refrained from giving publicity about the death. A legal aid lawyer investigating the death of Nakul Bagdi in December 1985 in Bihar said "A senior police officer ... came to me and advised me to drop the case. He advised me that since Nakul's brother had been given a job and since money had been raised privately for his father, it would be futile for FLAG [the legal aid committee] to pursue the case". Yet the post-mortem had stated clearly the body showed signs of physical assault.

Generally, witnesses and potential witnesses against the police have been subject to intimidation to prevent them testifying in criminal prosecutions of police officers. A lawyer representing Nakul Bagdi's family said that a police officer had told him: "nobody would give any adverse evidence against the police. And true enough, even the two youngsters who were picked up along with Nakul ... did not turn up to give evidence. They were virtually the eye-witnesses".

In fact, once evidence is found against the police, efforts are often made to reduce the severity of the charge. For example, charges of murder - carrying a punishment of life imprisonment or even death were initially brought against four Delhi police officers alleged to have tortured and killed Gopi Ram in August 1986. The Supreme Court found evidence of murder, but the charge was changed to the lesser one of endangering life or personal safety under Section 336 of the IPC, for which the maximum penalty is three months' imprisonment. According to one judge, charges against police officers are "diluted time and again".

Police inquiries are also often delayed for years as a means of evading punishment, as noted by *Amrita Bazar Patrika,* a Calcutta newspaper in September 1989. "Some of the cases are already three years old, and no one knows when they will end. By that time fresh cages will pile up and people will lose interest in the old cases and the fate of the culprits. The cases may then be wound up and the accused given a clean chit. There are many ways of sabotaging the process of justice, and prolonging police investigation is one of them."

To sum up, it can be safely surmised that policing and police system cannot be improved under a corrupt political system. So many declared criminals are now holding the posts of MLA's, M.P.', and other key posts in connivance of politicians, charged with corruption and other cases. Judiciary is also helpless, since vested interests are also present there. Convicted officials are acquitted. Though in recent past some top police officials are being tried and in jail in different parts of the country—but as politicians of dubious characters have been given clean chit, they will also be acquitted later or sooner.; As such there is no hope for a clean and transparent system unless and until collective and concerted efforts are made by the civil society to dilute and marginalise the corrpution and corrupt politicians.

[Note: The text of this chapter is based on the write-up of a distinguished scholar, I express gratefulness to him for subscribing his views.]

5

Custodial Violence: Causes & Concerns

"Your greatness is measured by your kindness— your education and intellect by your modesty—your ignorance is betrayed by your suspicions and prejudices— your real caliber is measured by the consideration and tolerance you have for others."

—*WM. J. H. Boetcker*

The incidents of police torture and brutality often hit the headlines in newspapers and expose police to severe criticisms from different sections of the society. Indeed nothing tarnishes the image of the police more than brutality directed against persons in their custody. Exposure of such incidents causes national and international concern. Amnesty International in its reports has been frequently making allegations regarding excessive use of force and torture by the Police in India. In its report in the year 1992, it mentioned that the number of deaths in police custody in India during the year 1985 to 1991 was 415. Though many of the allegations in the Report of Amnesty International remain unsubstantiated, the complaints of custodial violence and abuse of power by the Police cannot be brushed aside. There is a ring of truth in them. Even the official statistics will go to show that the malady does exist.

The charge of brutal custodial violence by the police often resulting in the death of the arrestees, is not new. Though allegations of custodial violence by the police are now coming to notice with increasing frequency, it will be good to remember that the evil is not of recent origin. It was, though not widely publicised, very much prevalent in the past. The commission for investigation of alleged cases of torture in the Madras Presidency in its report (1850) highlighted that police torture was quite prevalent in the then Madras Presidency. The Indian Police Commission (1902-03) had also written that "a serious complaint against the police is the unnecessary severity with which they often discharge their duty and the unnecessary annoyances they inflict on the public." The National Police Commission also analysed the evils of custodial rape and violence and suggested a number of corrective measures. Figures compiled by the National Crime Records Bureau show that during the year 1990-92 as many as 258 rapes and 197 deaths in police custody were reported from all over the country.

The National Human Rights Commission immediately after its constitution issued instruction (14th December 1993) to all District Magistrates and Superintendents of Police to report any incident of custodial death or rape directly to the Commission within 24 hours of the occurrence. Failure to send such reports, it was emphasised, will lead to a presumption by the commission that an effort was being made to suppress the occurrence. In the year 1995, 105 deaths in Police custody and 207 deaths in jail custody were also reported.

Of course, use of excessive force by the police against

persons in custody is not peculiar to India alone. Such allegations against the police are frequently levelled also, though that should not give room for •consolation or complacency, against police forces of advanced democratic countries. As early as in 1931. The National Crime Commission headed by Mr. George Wickersham, in the United States sharply criticized the police department for routine use of torture and third-degree methods. In 1966, the President's Commission on Law Enforcement and Administration of Justice came across several incidents in which the police used unnecessary force and violence. The recent incident of custodial violence of Los Angeles policemen against Rodney King resulted in large-scale riots in many cities in the USA.

Charges of custodial violence have also been levelled against the police in the United Kingdom including the famous Scotland Yard. Even before a Royal Commission printed its report on police behaviour in 1960, scandals began to occur that tarnished the pristine police image. A "rhino whip" was discovered in a Sheffield locker and a London detective, Harry Challoner, was dismissed for planting evidence. A well-organised "firm within a firm" was revealed to permeate the structure of the detectives in the Metropolitan Police reaching, right upto the top, including the elite Flying Squad.

Unfortunately, reports of police violence and brutality, received from various parts of the country, convey an impression that the police forces in our country are full of sadists and bloodthirsty maniacs who relish the sight of broken skulls and blinded eyes. But this prevalent impression is misleading. Majority of police officers and men are not cruel sadists and do possess a certain degree of commitment and motivation which enable them to stand the stress and strain of their difficult and thankless job Of course, there are some who, in the confines of the police stations or police barracks, do not hesitate to inflict unspeakable torture on the arrestees.

An Inspector of Orissa Police posted in Koraput district who brutally kicked to death in the police station a bright school boy when the latter at the time of interrogation, had the temerity to ask him that under which section of law he had the authority to misbehave or use third-degree methods during the investigation of a case. The Inspector's blood was up. He gave two hard kicks with his boots on the chest of the boy and two in his genitals. The poor boy gave a loud shriek and breathed his last. The Inspector then tried with the help of the police station staff to show it as a case of suicide by hanging the body from a nearby electric pole. The investigation done by the, CID team, sent from State Police Headquarters unravelled the truth. The Inspector was prosecuted u/s 302 IPC for murder. But the Sessions Judge in a mood of clemency exonerated the officer of the charge of murder and convicted him under section 323 IPC for causing, hurt. But nemesis overtook him. He soon lost his life in a road accident.

Despite elaborate legal provisions fettering exercise of arbitrary authority by the police, and detailed instruction in the State Police Manuals prohibiting abuse of powers by police personnel while effecting arrests or interrogating suspects or accused at any stage of investigation of a case, many a, police officer develops a feeling that he can get away with the worst forms of custodial violence because it will be very difficult to prove such a charge as none will come forward to give evidence. He also feels that his superiors and subordinates will rally round him and try to whitewash his omissions or commissions.

Custodial deaths thus generate more heat than light. Every such death is not probed into on systematic lines. The National Police Commission (1977) analysed complaints of police torture and custodial deaths in eight states and found that the police were blamed in 11 out of 17 judicial enquiries, 37 out of 82 magisterial enquiries and 23 out of 430 enquiries by other agencies. The National Police Commission recommended that in all cases of custodial deaths there should be mandatory judicial inquiries.

Causes of Custodial Crimes

One of the causes of custodial deaths is the tremendous pressure on the police to detect cases whenever there is a surge in crime, and particularly heinous crime. Whenever crime increases, it is the police which is singled out for, blame.

The popular and prevalent notion is that efficiency or inefficiency of the police is the decisive factor behind any increase or reduction in crime. The fact is forgotten that crime is a result of various socioeconomic factors over which the police have no control. Again the resources of the police-manpower, equipment and gadgets—are totally inadequate and they function under various legal impediments.

The impact of the pressure is mostly felt at the subordinate levels who are required to deliver the goods in quick time. It is a curious anomaly that while law gives power to police officer to arrest anyone and keep him under custody for atleast 24 hours, it places unreasonable restrictions on the testimony of the police officers.

Sections 161, 162, 164 of CrPC and Sections 25, 26, 27 of the Indian Evidence Act should be recast to remove shackles on police testimony. Section 162, CrPC provides that the maker of statement before the police is not to sign it. This frequently enables the witnesses to resile from the statements they have made before the police in courts of law. In England and in many other advanced democratic countries, statements before the police are generally signed and considerable importance is attached to them because it is difficult to confute such statements. Of course, judges, should always have discretionary powers to exclude evidence which, they think, has been unfairly or coereively obtained. Lord Devlin in 'Criminal Prosecution in England' , has very aptly observed that since the police force cannot be excluded altogether from the field of investigation, and since the worst thing of all is to have an irresponsible police force, is it not better to leave the police in sole charge of enquiry and to ensure that they act under a sense of responsibility to the Court for what they do?

Under law the police can detain a person in custody for 24 hours. After that he is to be produced before the magistrate. Very often, the court does not grant any further police custody. If a notorious criminal is quickly bailed out, it is difficult to trace him out again. To circumvent the law, a new procedure is being increasingly adopted by the police whereby a suspect is being, picked up and detained for Many days. No permission is sought from the court and no information is given to the relatives regarding the whereabouts of the detainee. Even if the detainee dies, the police do not own responsibility as there is no evidence to show that he died in police custody.

The stark fact also cannot be gainsaid that there is some amount of double-thinking and double-speaking over the issue. Even enlightened members of the society expect police to take 'tough action" not sanctioned by law against antisocial elements who are escaping conviction and getting away scot-free because of the malfunctioning of the criminal justice system. In a case of gruesome double murder which created consternation in Cuttack, a responsible political leader suggested to utilise all kinds of techniques known to a police officer to elicit information from the suspect. Unfortunately, many officers opt fur short-cut, rough-and-ready methods for quick results.

Subordinate officers who are entrusted with the job of applying third-degree methods overdo it. Custodial deaths often occur not because of any intention to kill the victim, but as a result of excessive torture or when, quite unknowingly, the officer injures some weak organ in the victim's anatomy.

Again it is important to remember that such abuses of police can flourish not only because of official negligence or acquiescence but because, rightly or wrongly, broad sections of people under certain conditions and circumstances feel that the police, in spite of their excesses, are carrying out a necessary and unpleasant task for preserving and protecting state and society.

Such conditions place considerable moral burdens on conscientious police officials whose actions to check drifts of this kind are of paramount importance. A perceptive writer on Police Psychology, Ben Whitaker ('Police') has observed, the public "Janus-like have always turned two faces towards a policeman." Because of incompatible demands of the public, some policemen become stoically immune to criticism.

It is a fact that officers of police stations who do most of the investigations are a hard-pressed, hard-worked and beleaguered lot. An analysis of the National Police Commission shows that an investigating officer is able to devote only 37 percent of his time in investigational work while the rest of his time is taken up by other duties connected with maintenance of V.I.P. bandobust, petition enquiries, court attendance etc.

The result is farewell to open and painstaking investigation and dependence on short-cut, extra-legal methods and torture. For success of thorough investigation permitted under laws and rules an increase of the investigation staff and separation of the law and order and investigation staff is absolutely necessary. This suggestion has been made by expert bodies like Law Commission of India and various Police Commissions. This will, however, necessitate substantially larger recruitment of policemen to cope with the heavy workload.

It is necessary in this connection to bear in mind another aspect of police functioning. There are informal rules of police subculture which glorify deviance not in terms of personal gain or aggrandizement, but as a requirement for completing the police jobs. Several studies have highlighted the unfortunate situation in police organizations which engender a belief in newly recruited officers that what they have been taught in training school is to be quickly unlearned and they must fall in line with the prevalent culture in the organization in which the emphasis is on the end of apprehending and convicting criminals and not on the means to be adopted to attain the objective. It is a fact that the victims of custodial violence mostly are people coining from poor and backward sections of the society with little political or financial power to back them. Personal enmity, caste and political considerations, and at times pecuniary benefits become important considerations for custodial deaths rather than investigation of cases.

To prevent custodial violence it is necessary for, senior officers of the force to make clear to the subordinates that use of third-degree methods against persons in custody will not be condoned and swift and deterrent action will be taken against the perpetrators of such offences. Superior officers from the Superintendent of Police to the D.G. first must themselves realise that third degree methods are criminal offences made punishable by Indian Penal Code vide Sections 330 and 331. They must send clear and unequivocal signals to the subordinates that if any case of torture to persons detained in custody comes to notice, they will take deterrent action against the offenders. Unfortunately, many senior officers tacitly encourage these aberrations, and then blame the subordinates when things get out of hand. This kind of duplicitous approach will not help, This only creates a feeling among the subordinate staff that senior officers are paying lip-service to laws and rules and they do not really mean what they preach. Again it is seen that through in a large number of cases of custodial deaths officers responsible are suspended and departmental enquiries instituted, such departmental enquiries drag on and ultimately very few offenders are brought to book.

During surprise visits to the policestations, the senior officers must ensure that police station officers keep correct, up-to-date and true records of persons called for questioning and enquiry and the records should contain details of reasons for such action. These records are to be verified to ensure that persons in detention are not subjected to inhuman treatment or torture. It has been very perceptively observed by Professor Twining (Benthem on torture) that institutionalization of torture would lead to the "creation of a guild of professional torturers and would open the door for steady erosion of resistance to it in less extreme cases until ordinary people become conditioned to accept it as commonplace and tolerable."

The National Police Commission in its First Report (February, 1979) clearly recommended mandatory judicial enquiry in the case of an alleged rape, death or grievous injury in police custody. It added that such a judicial enquiry should be held by an Additional Sessions Judge nominated for the purpose who could be designated as the District Inquiry Authority DIA. The DIA could be assisted by an assessor who can be an Additional S.P. or a senior DSP nominated for this purpose in each district or a group of districts. DIA's enquiry will be in the nature of fact-finding and his report will go to the State Government which would take appropriate action in consulation with the Police Chief. This recommendation of the NPC is sound and pragmatic. The association of a Judge with the enquiry from its inception will give it a certain amount of credibility. At the same time co-option of a police officer will ensure that police version also gets proper attention and scrutiny. It is unfortunate that this valuable recommendation of the NPC has not been implemented.

As many arrested persons in police custody in a state of acute mental depression commit suicide, it is necessary for the senior officers visiting the police station to see that no weapons or articles that can facilitate escape or suicide like bamboos, ropes, tools, etc. are within the reach of the lock-up. Indeed the Police Manuals of various States have elaborate rules for the sale custody and protection of prisoners in the lockup. Any wilful breach of these rules are made punishable with imprisonment or fine under Section 29 of the Indian Police Act, 1861.

The Law Commission of India, on a reference made by the Supreme Court of India, recommended (June, 1985) that a Section 114(B) should be inserted in the Indian Evidence Act, 1872, to introduce a rebuttable presumption that injuries's sustained by a person in police custody may be presumed to have been caused by the police officer. Such a provision perhaps will have a restraining effect on officers indulging in torture. Similarly, amendments in CrPC provides for examination of the arrested by a medical practitioner at the request of the latter. It should be amended to provide for compulsory physical examination of the arrested person by a medical practitioner with a detailed record of his physical and mental condition. A time has also come to think of adequate compensation to the victims. At present there is no law governing the liability of State for the wrong done to the citizen by the a public servant in course of his employment. The only provision regarding payment of compensation is contained in CrPC Section 357 which provides for payment of compensation for a loss or injury caused by criminal offence to the victim after, the fine is imposed by the court. The provision crimes or family members in many cases. In the case of Rudul Sah V State of Bihar, while awarding interim compensation for wrongful detention, the Supreme Court observed that "respect for rights of individuals is the bastion of democracy.

Therefore, the state must repair the damage done by its officers to the petitioner's rights." However, the amount of compensation has not been uniform and cardinal principles have not been laid down. It is desirable to frame a suitable legislation under which the State should pay compensation to the victims of custodial crime or to their kith and kin. During the training of the Indian Police Service -officers at the National Police Academy there is constant emphasis on sensitizing them to the issues of human rights and making clear that extra-legal methods are counter-productive. In all police training institutions in the country there should be constant emphasis on the fact that no explanation or expediency can justify the use of torture.

It is necessary to provide more powers to facilitate investigation by the Police, but at the same time it has to be strictly ensured that powers are not misused. In Kishor Singh V State of Rajasthan (A.I.R. 1982 SC 625) the Supreme Court observed, "Nothing is more cowardly and unconscionable than a person in police custody being beaten up and nothing inflicts a deeper wound in our constitutional culture than a State official running berserk regardless of human rights" has to be read and re-read by the police trainers. Again, international opinion in the form of Conventions and Covenants has declared that the right not to be tortured is a non-derogable right. India is a signatory to the Universal Declaration of Human Rights and the International Covenant on Civil and Political Rights and is thus under an international obligation to see that the non-derogable right of freedom from torture is not violated. Further, Article 2 of the United Nations Code of Conduct for Law Enforcement Officials categorically lays down that in the performance of their duty, law-enforcement officials shall respect and protect human dignity and maintain and uphold the human rights of all persons.

There should also be constant exhortation by the senior officers in the field to the members of the force at the cutting-edge levels that extra-legal methods and torture are self-defeating and will expose them to legal and departmental action.

While examining ways, and means of making laws more humanistic and providing safeguards against abuse of power by the police, it is also necessary to bear in mind, at the same time, the difficult conditions under which the police are functioning. Some of the legal impediments that hamper proper functioning of the police are to be removed. This is needed more so at a time when the police are confronting unprecedented problems of law and order. Detention in police custody for 24 hours before sending the accused to court is a check on arbitrary abuse of authority by the police. But it does create problems in investigation of complicated cases where, sustained interrogation in police custody is necessary to unearth vital clues and elicit more information. It can be mentioned in this connection that in UK the Prevention of Terrorism Act, 1974, permits the police to arrest without warrant for offences under the Act and detain the suspect for 48 hours and for a further 5 days with the Home Secretary's approval. The creation of the National Human Rights Commission by the Government has been welcomed by all sections including the police. It provides a forum where complaints against violation of human rights can be aired. The creation of the Commission by the Government has sent correct signals to members of the police that violations of human rights will not be brooked by the Government. It also, at the same time, provides an opportunity to the police to demolish false and motivated allegations.

ROLE OF SUPREME COURT

Role of law and human rights are intimately interrelated concepts. Rule of law is the basis for the governance of human society. Whenever we talk of upholding Rule of Law, we visualize a system of justice which accepts and respects the basic rights of the individuals. If a society fails to evolve an effective machinery for protecting human rights its edifice of democracy will suffer cracks and in the long-run a 'Rule of Jungle' will operate to perish it.

The incidence of lock-up death has increased in the recent past. In many cases lock-up deaths are the result of third degree methods adopted by the police during interrogation of prisoners.

In *Raghubir Singh v. State of Haryana,* theft had been committed in some officers' houses. Some suspects had been picked up by the police. Suspects were tortured and one of them died. Trial Court convicted the sub-Inspector of Police for life imprisonment. Supreme Court confirmed the decision of the trial court. Supreme Court observed:

> We are deeply disturbed by the diabolical recurrence of police torture resulting in a terrible scare in the minds of common citizens ... when the guardians of law become the violators of human rights.'"

In *State of U.P. v. Ram Sagar Yadav,* one Brijlal made a complaint to Superintendent of Police that a police constable had demanded bribe from him. Brijlal was brought to the police station and then tortured to death for having dared to make such a complaint, Supreme Court convicted the police man under Section 302 of I.P.C.

Similar decision was pronounced by the Supreme Court in *Gauri Shankar Sharma's* case where one Ram Dhiraj was beaten to death in police lock-up. Supreme Court observed:

Death in police custody must be seriously viewed for otherwise we will be taking a stride in the direction of police raj.

State Liability for Lock-up Deaths

No doubt lock-up deaths lead to a clear violation of Article 21 of the Constitution, yet the Apex Court has through its leading, judgments, apart from convicting the guilty police officials, also sought to grant compensation for illegal detentions and lock-up deaths.

In *Rudul Shah v.* Union *of India,* the petitioner was

illegally detained for 14 years in Ranchi Jail of Bihar. After his acquittal, Chief Justice Chanderchud said that one of the effective ways of preventing violation of Article 21 was to make the violators pay compensation, In *Bhim Singh v. State of J&K* the court awarded Rs. 50,000 as compensation to Bhim. Singh who had been illegally detained for delivering an inflammatory speech in Sept. 1985.

In *Saheli v. Commissioner of Police* the Supreme Court awarded Rs. 75,000 as compensation to Mrs. Kamlesh Kumari whose 9 year old son was beaten to death by the Delhi Police officials and directed to recover the amount from the erring, police officials.

In *State of Maharashtra v. Ravikanth,* the Supreme Court held that delinquent police officers could not be made personally liable to pay compensation.

In *Nilabati Behra v. Union of India,* the Supreme Court held that the real threat to rule of law came from the growing lawlessness of the State functionaries particularly the police and wherever there was, contravention of human rights and fundamental rights, there was an enforceable right to compensation. There are numerous other cases wherein the Supreme Court and different High Courts have shown a lot of judicial awareness towards protection of individual rights and liberties. In the light of the above discussion the various points that need the consideration are listed below:

(a) Constitution does not guarantee a right to compensation for violations of human rights. Such a right should be specifically incorporated in the Constitution.

(b) In many cases the States have sought from liability to pay compensation by seeking refuge under the doctrines of 'Sovereign Immunity in torts. It is submitted that this outdated distinction between sovereign and non-sovereign functions of the state should be done away with and state should not be exempted from liability in such situations.

(c) 'Custodial death' should be defined and made a crime inviting stringent punishment under I.P.C.

(d) Who is to pay Compensation' - The State or the guilty police official - One view is that the delinquent police officer should be made personally liable and the state should be finally resolved.

(e) A new concept of 'Encounter Deaths' is fast emerging as the police is arming itself with vast powers to deal with the threat of terrorism. This concept needs to be defined and concretised and the ambit of the exercise of police powers in the light of that definition demarcated.

(f) Legal requirement of production of arrested person before the Magistrate within 24 hours is generally not observed in case of custodial crimes. Victims of such crimes are not shown to have been arrested. This arbitrary and unjust exercise of police powers needs to be bridled.

(g) Commission of 'Custodial Crimes' may raise a presumption that 'General Diary" meant for recording events and proceedings at a police station is not being maintained properly. In a reported case of lock-up death, the courts should scrutinize the General Diary to ascertain the complicity of the police official in the crime.

(h) Law Commission recommendation that when death occurs in custody, it should be presumed that it was not due to natural causes should be accorded statutory recognition.

(i) Can we deny that there is something wrong with the training imparted to members of police force that instead of inculcating a feeling of confidence and protection in the minds of lay persons, their presence and strategy of operation is striking terror and disgust in the community?

(j) Experience of the working of our political system holds ample testimony to the fact that at times there is an active involvement of political figures wielding enormous powers, in using the machinery of police to gag the voice of dissent or opposition to paralysis the system for the aggrandisement of their vested interests.

CAUSES AND CURES TO CUSTODIAL VIOLENCE

The Constitution of India and the International Instruments on Human Rights attach great importance to the protection of life and personal liberty of an individual and emphasise the respect for human dignity. Our Basic Law and the substantive and procedural laws stress the need to observe human rights in the administration of criminal justice.

Arrest involves the deprivation of the liberty of an individual by legal authorities. From the time a person is arrested, if not released on bail, he or she is under custody. Any use of force, threat, psychological pressure etc., against the person in custody by the authorities is termed as custodial violence. We have seen the basic legal philosophy of the Constitution, the international instruments and the procedural law, which presume the innocence of the accused till the contrary is proved in a court of law. Keeping this in view, the legal procedures are weighted in favour of the accused and his innocence. Custodial violence takes place due to social, psychological, professional and administrative factors. Sometimes it also takes place due to, psychological aberrations of the custodian: sadism, sexual weaknesses, social hatreds etc.

Causes

Social factors: In our country, we are accustomed to think in terms of "an eye for an eye and a tooth for a tooth". Therefore, society tacitly expects and approves of the use, of violence on suspects to get at the truth. Complainants themselves, particularly in property offences, incite the police to use force or violence to reak" a suspect. Therefore, in a society where the public is indifferent to the use of force, on fellow human beings, policemen get, as it were, social support for these illegal acts. Frequently, reports appearing in the press about lynching and stoning to death of alleged thieves, child lifters, sorcerers etc., reflect the state of mind of Indian society on this issue. Thus, there is no social stigma attached to the use of custodial violence by the police.

Psychological Factors: Stories of brutalities indulged in by the police, in all their unsavoury details, circulate widely among the public, including members of the underworld. Though many of these stories may be the product of fertile imagination, the fact remains that the general public believe them to be true. Therefore, when a suspect is picked up for interrogation by the police, he anticipates "full police treatment" and is apprehensive of his physical safety, Any use of force or even a threat to use force breaks him down completely and he Is prepared to come dean. Due to this fear psychosis, petty criminals, on many occasions, are known to admit their complicity in heinous crimes in which they had no part at all. Unscrupulous police officials tend to play on this fear psychosis and freely use violence to obtain confessions.

Professional and Administrative Factors

(a) In normal police work, law and order takes priority and the prevention and detection of crime gets only secondary attention. To be a successful detective, a Police Station House Officer should have a thorough knowledge of his jurisdiction; the incidence and pattern of crimes; the modus operandi and other details of the criminals residing in his area; full details of harbourers and receivers of stolen property; and complete knowledge of undesirable and antisocial elements of the area. To acquire this knowledge, the officer should have sufficient time and leisure at his disposal. Unfortunately, with his preoccupation with law and order duties, he is not able to concentrate on this important aspect of his work. Thus, his approach to crime work tends to be unsystematic and unscientific.

(b) Interrogation of a suspect is a battle of wits. It presupposes superior knowledge and wisdom on the part of the interrogator. He needs, in addition to full possession of facts and figures, enough time at his disposal. Under the law of our country, a suspect has to be produced in court within 24 hours. Courts are reluctant to grant 'police remand. Thus, the interrogator is forced to work against time. He is prepared to adopt any short-cut method to gain time. In sensational cases, subordinate police officers are subjected to tremendo is pressure from their departmental superiors, the press and the public to produce quick results. In the absence of professional expertise and lack of time, custodial violence presents itself as a panacea for the interrogator and the investigating officer to obtain quick results.

(c) Legal hurdles like the inability to keep a suspect for longer than a day, the Evidence Act being weighed against the police etc., are factors which induce the police to keep Suspects in unofficial custody. Once a Suspect is in unofficial Custody, he ceases as such to exist on record, for the purposes of law. What is done to him is known only to police officials within the precincts of a police station. This helps and encourages the police to indulge in custodial violence with impunity.

While custodial violence is common in the sphere of crime investigation to extract information/confession about crime and to recover property etc., it also occurs in maintenance of order situations particularly while dealing with political violence like terrorism, extremism etc. Unable to face the pressure from political extremists and in the absence of legal remedies to neutralise them, the police often indulge in elimination of adversaries through illegal methods.

The law has prohibited the use of custodial violence in unmistakable terms. The Indian Penal Code makes it an offence to voluntarily cause hurt to extort confession or to compel restoration of property. The Constitution of India gives the fundamental right to the citizen not to be compelled to be a witness against himself. The Criminal Procedure Code prohibits offering of threats, promises or inducements to extract information, The. Indian Evidence Act prohibits the use of confession made before a Police Officer and the one obtained through inducement, threat or promise, in criminal trials. The Indian Penal Code makes it an offence to wrongfully confine a person to extract confession or compel restoration of property. The Indian Police Act, under which the entire police organisation in India derives its legitimacy and the policeman his powers to function, prohibits unwarranted personal violence by police officers to any person in police custody, The Indian Penal Code lays down minimum punishment for rapes occurring in police custody. There are punitive procedures both administrative and judicial, in case of complaints of custodial violence against police officers.

Thus, it is dear that custodial, violence is illegal and policemen who are to uphold the law cannot indulge in illegal acts. Custodial Violence undermines human dignity, brutalises the police system, forfeits the trust of the people and the judiciary and also affects the image of police organisation as a whole Finally, It also exposes the police officer to the risk of criminal liability and punishment.

In spite of these clear legal prohibitions and negative aspects, the police indulge in custodial violence due to the erroneous belief that it is a short Cut to Success Studies prove that custodial violence is counter-productive and does not add in any significant way to the achievement of the goals and objectives of the police organisation. Further, investigation of crime is a battle of wits with the criminal and calls for sustained and prolonged efforts on the part of police. As pressure of work mounts, custodial violence is resorted to, to achieve crime control objectives. While crime does not pay, neither do custodial violence.

In situations of political violence, elimination of adversaries through "fake encounters" only strengthens the cause of the adversaries. The public gets alienated from the State and their non-cooperation with the authorities strengthens the cause of the rebels. The root cause of political violence is political in nature and the cures should also be political in nature. The police should confine themselves to fighting the criminality involved in the actions of the rebels and, through better tactical and professional skills and methods, attempt to neutralise them. To fight the rebels one needs information and cooperation from the public. Custodial violence takes the people away from the police and weakens their efforts to get information.

The Supreme Court of India and various State High Courts have condemned custodial violence and spoken strongly against it. They have proposed stringent punishment for custodial violence. The Supreme Court has observed: "The Police, with their wide powers are apt to overstep their zeal to detect crimes and are tempted to use the strong arm against those who happen to fall under their secluded jurisdiction. That tendency and that temptation must, in the larger interest of justice, be nipped in the bud."

Cures

Central Reception Facility for Arrestees

The bulk of arrests are made in cities and towns, Efforts must therefore be concentrated in these areas.

All persons taken into custody in a city or town should be brought to a central reception facility, which should be under the direct charge of a senior gazetted police officer. All arrestees should be subjected to a thorough medical examination and a record of the same should be kept, Further, every arrestee should be given a pamphlet in the vernacular, listing out his rights and his acknowledgement obtained. If the arrestee is an illiterate, the same should be read over to him and the official doing so should make a record to this effect. In case of arrestees suffering from custodial shock, trauma and depression, the assistance of a psychiatrist should be made available. Arrestees should be held over in the central reception facility till produced in court or until they are remanded to police custody by the courts.

Special investigation rooms with modern facilities should be available to enabled the investigating officers to carry on further interrogation of the arrestees, All movements of the, arrestees, during their stay in the central reception facility should be recorded. Separate accommodation for women and juveniles should be provided and an adequate number of women police officers should be available to take charge of them. Consequent on the establishment of a central reception facility, there would be no need for lock-ups in police stations and the holding of prisoners in police stations should be prohibited.

Duty judicial Magistrate

A judicial magistrate should be available round the clock at a designated place in the city or town, to attend to the judicial needs of the arrestees. He should be vested with all powers to grant bail, record confessions, issue judicial process, etc. His presence and availability will automatically reduce the need for the police to hold the arrestees overnight or when the courts are closed.

Need to Review Powers of Arrest

With the enactment of a plethora of social, fiscal and other laws, the powers of the police to arrest have widened beyond imagination. This gives scope for misbehaviour and avoidable custody. A review of these powers of arrest is called for and suitable corrective steps are to be taken.

Escort of Prisoners

Transportation of prisoners by public transport and escorting them by unarmed police constables should be prohibited. The prisoners should be transported in proper secure prison vehicles and should be escorted by armed policemen only. Courts should have specially earmarked spaces to accommodate the prisoners attending the courts.

The police in India are required to register all crime and investigate most of them. Their performance is judged by the rate of convictions obtained by them and by the quantum of property recovered from the criminals. Most cases of Custodial violence are related to property offences and are resorted to obtain confessions and to recover property. A resetting of the goals and levels of performance in police organisation in respect of property offences would automatically reduce the scope for custodial violence.

Complaint Boards

To look into and verify complaints of custodial deaths, a Police Complaints board, consisting of a retired district and sessions judge (chairman) and a retired police officer of the rank of superintendent of police and a prominent senior citizen with administrative background as members, should visit the scene and ascertain the facts. If, in its opinion, a prima facie case exists, a direction should be issued to the local chief of police to register a criminal case against the police personnel concerned and hand over the case to the Crime Branch, CID, for further investigation,

Whenever a death occurs in police custody, a judicial enquiry by the district and sessions judge should become mandatory.

A sustained publicity campaign should be undertaken to educate the public and the police about the sanctity of human rights. This should be a positive campaign and not a negative one to denigrate the police. Instead of concentrating on custodial violence only, this campaign should speak in terms of the rights of women, children, the schedule castes, the scheduled tribes and others and protection from unlawful custody and violence while under custody should be brought in as part of the general picture. This is to ensure that the police do not feel that they have been singled out for denigration in public. In all police publications, an advertisement regarding human rights should be carried. The electronic media should be used extensively, Such a campaign is necessary as the police force, with a strength of about ten lakhs, is spread out in small groups all over the country and it is not easy to reach them to sensitise them on this issue.

Custodial violence is anathema in any civilized society. Law enforcement agencies, particularly the police, should make a conscious effort to banish this evil practice from their organisations. Till this is done, the police will not earn the respect and co-operation of the public and find a honourable place for themselves in society.

6

Police Atrocities and Judicial Measures

" A thing that you sincerely believe in, cannot be wrong. Because belief does not come at will. It comes only from the Holy Ghost within. Therefore a thing you really believe in cannot be wrong."

—*D. H. Lawrence,*
Studies in Classical American Litera-ture

International Commitments

One of the important purposes of the U.N. Charter is to promote and encourage human rights and fundamental freedom. Human rights are part and parcel of "human dignity" and the importance of the concept of "human dignity" is well exemplified by its inclusion in the Universal Declaration of Human Rights; International Covenant on Economic, Social and Cultural Rights and the International Covenant on Civil and Political Rights:

Article 3 of the Universal Declaration of Human Rights provides:

- Everyone has the right to life, liberty and security.
- Article 5 of the Declaration provides:
- No one shall be subjected to torture or to cruel, inhuman or degrading treatment or punishment.

Further right to equality before law and right to effective remedy for acts violating the fundamental right, have been guaranteed. Article 9 of the Declaration provides:

- No one shall be subjected to arbitrary arrest, detention or exile.

Everyone is entitled in full equality to a fair and public hearing by an independent and impartial tribunal, in the determination of his rights and obligations and of any criminal charge against him. Everyone charged with a penal offence has the right to be presumed innocent until proved guilty according to law in a public trial at which he has had all the guarantees necessary for his defence. No one shall be held guilty of any penal offence on account of any act or omission which did not constitute a penal offence under national or international law, at the time when it was committed.

Similarly, Article 6(1) of the International Covenant on Civil and Political Rights provides:

- Every human being has the inherent right to life. This right shall be protected by law. No one shall be arbitrarily deprived of his life.

Article 7 of the International Covenant, on Civil and Political Right further provides:

- No one shall be subjected to torture or to cruel, inhuman or degrading treatment or punishment. In particular, no one shall be subjected without his free consent to medical or scientific experimentation.

It may be noted that Article 7 of the Covenant is a non-derogable provision. It has been further provided that everyone has the right to liberty and security of person. No one shall be subjected to arbitrary arrest or detention. No one shall be deprived of his liberty except on such grounds and in accordance with such procedure as are established by law.

Adequate protections against arrest and detention have been ensured under the Covenant and in case anyone has been victim of unlawful arrest or detention, then he shall have an enforceable right to compensation. It is, further provided that all persons deprived of their liberty shall be treated with humanity and with respect for inherent dignity of the human person. The right of fair hearing and equality before the Courts has also been guaranteed. Article 15 of the Covenant prohibits the enactment of retrospective Criminal Law. And this provision is also non-derogable.

In addition to this, there are Standard Minimum Rules for the Treatment of Prisoners; Declaration on the Protection of all persons from Being Subjected to Torture and Other Cruel, Inhuman or Degrading Treatment or Punishment;' Convention against Torture and Other Cruel, Inhuman or Degrading Treatment or Punishment and Code of Conduct for Law Enforcement Officials.

Constitutional Mandates

Article 20 of the Indian Constitution provides safeguards to the persons accused of crimes, against *ex post facto* law, double jeopardy and prohibits self-incrimination, Article 21 of the Constitution provides:

> No person shall be deprived of his life or personal liberty except according to the procedure established by law.

This provision advances the object of Article 3 of the Universal Declaration of Human Rights and Article 6 of the International Covenant on Civil and Political Rights.

The judiciary has expanded the scope and ambit of Article 21 of the Constitution. In *Maneka Gandhi v. Union of India,* the Supreme Court held that "the expression 'personal liberty' in Article 21 is of the widest amplitude and it covers a variety of rights which go to constitute the personal liberty of men and some of them have been raised to the status of distinct fundamental rights and given additional protection under Article 19 (of the Constitution)". The right to live under Article 21 is not confined merely to physical existence or animal existence but it includes within its ambit the "right to live with human dignity".

In Jolly *George Varghese v. Bank of Cochin, it* was observed:

> The High value of human dignity and the worth of human person enshrined in Article 21 read with Articles 14 and 19, obligates the State to incarcerate except under law which is fair, just and reasonable in its procedural essence.

In *Kishore Singh v. State of Rajasthan, the* Supreme Court once again pointed out:

> Human dignity is a clear value of our Constitution not to be bartered away for mere apprehensions by jail officials.

The right to "personal liberty" under Article 21 of the Constitution is of widest amplitude and it provides protection against police atrocities in various forms. Article 21 of the Constitution covers, *inter alia,* the right against solitary confinement, the right against bar fitters, the right to legal aid; the right against handcuffing; the right against custodial violence and protection against use of third degree methods by the police.

Article 22 of the Constitution deals with protection against arrest and detention in certain cases. In fact, Article

22 of the Constitution supplements Article 21. Article 22 prescribes the minimum procedural requirements that must be included in any law enacted by the legislature in accordance with which a person may be deprived of his life or personal liberty. The talk of human rights and declaring them as fundamental rights in the Constitution is meaningless unless they can be enforced by an effective machinery.

If there is no effective remedy against the violation of human rights, there *is* no effective human right in the real sense. Article 32 of the Constitution provides remedy for the enforcement of the fundamental rights. The judiciary in India has done matchless service in protecting the people from police atrocities and thus protected their human rights.

Police Atrocities and Judicial Wisdom

Policemen stepping out of the legal boundaries is not new; but the frequency and the freedom with which they trample on the rights of the citizens are frightening. As the Supreme Court has said, the police has come to treat itself as law unto itself, sometimes even above the law.. It is heart-rending to note that day in and day out we come across with the news of blood-curdling incidents of police brutality and atrocities, alleged to have been committed, in utter disregard and in all breaches of humanitarian law and universal human rights as well as total negation of the Constitutional guarantees and human decency. When the police becomes an irresponsible lot, the plight of the people becomes deplorable.

The Courts, which arc expected to intervene in an exceptional cases, are having to do so on an almost daily basis. Instead of shaming the police into action, this is being construed as judicial activism with all its consequences.

Imprisonment does not spell farewell to fundamental

rights. In *Sunil Batra (1) v. Delhi Admn., the* Apex Court observed:

Part III of the Constitution *does* not part company with the prisoners at the gates, and judicial oversight protects the prisoner's shrinken fundamental rights, if flouted, frowned upon or frozen by the prison authority:

In *Sunil Batra (11) v. Delhi Admn.,* the human rights conscious Court expressed its concern against the police atrocities over putting fetters in the following words:

> (T)o fetter prisoners in irons is an inhumanity unjustified save where safe custody is otherwise impossible. The routine resort to handcuffs and irons bespeaks a barbarity hostile to our goal of human dignity and social justice.

In *Kishore Singh v. State* of *Rajasthan, the* Apex Court showed its deep concern regarding the police atrocities in the following words:

> (N)o police life-style which relies more on fists than on wits, on torture more than on culture can control crime because means boomerang on ends and re-fuel the vice which it seeks to extinguish. Secondly, the State must re-educate the Constabulary out of their sadistic arts and inculcate a respect for human person - a process which must begin more by example than by precept if the lower rungs are really to emulate... Nothing is more cowardly and unconscionable than a person in police custody being beaten up and nothing inflicts a deeper wound on our Constitutional culture than a State official running berserk regardless of human rights.

The Supreme Court has always reacted against the police for handcuffing a person. In *Prem Shankar v. Delhi Admn.,*

Justice Krishna Iyer held that handcuffs should not be used in routine and they were to be used only when the person was "desperate ", "rowdy" or the one who was involved in non-bailable offence. He rightly observed:

> Handcuffing is *prima-facie* inhuman and, therefore, unreasonable, is overharsh and at the first blush, arbitrary. Absent fair procedure and objective monitoring to inflict 'irons' is to resort to zoological strategies repugnant to Article 21.

Despite the eye opening judgements of the Supreme Court against handcuffing, the police has been resorting to handcuffing in subsequent cases, The high headedness of the police authorities came to the light in *Delhi Judicial Service Asson., Tis Hazari Court v. State of Gujarat,"* (popularly known *as Nadiad* case). The case exhibited the berserk behaviour of police undermining the dignity and independence of judiciary. In this case the inspector of police of Nadiad police station arrested, assaulted and handcuffed the Chief Judicial Magistrate of Nadiad town and tied him with a thick rope like an animal with the object of humiliating him as he had been policing the police by his judicial orders.

The Supreme Court took serious note of the whole incident and laid down detailed guidelines which are to be followed in case of arrest and detention of a judicial officer. The guilty police inspector was given the simple imprisonment for a period of six months and was also directed to pay a fine of Rs. 2000. The court also sent other guilty police officials to jail and imposed fine and further directed the State Government to take disciplinary action against them.

It is submitted that whenever any police official acts contrary to the clear directions against handcuffing as laid down by the Supreme Court and thus violates the basic human rights to "human dignity", he should be made personally liable to pay the compensation.

In *State of Maharashtra v. Ravikant, where* an under-trial prisoner was handcuffed and taken through streets in a procession by police during investigation, the Court held it to be violative of Article 21 of the Constitution and directed the State to pay Rs. 10,000 to the under-trial prisoner. However, the Court held that since the police officer was acting in his "official capacity" so he cannot be made personally liable to pay the compensation. It is submitted that police authorities while acting in official capacity cannot take law in their own hands and whenever their action amounts to violation of human rights of the people they should be made personally liable to pay the compensation and suitable action should be taken against them.

Recently, in *Khedat Mazdoor Chetna Sangath v. State of* M. P., human rights violation by handcuffing of tribals and commission of inhuman atrocities on them by police officials and local administration was alleged by the petitioner tribal organisation. Though the allegations were not proved by sufficient evidence yet the Court by observing that the police has not recorded the happening faithfully and misrepresented locking up of six persons, held that handcuffing is illegal end to uphold human values and to protect the rights guaranteed under the Constitution it was further directed that C.B.I, should investigate and register cases and prosecute the guilty officials, howsoever high or low.

It is submitted that the Supreme Court has taken the right approach in this, case. The basic question is who will police the police? The government should pay serious attention to any possibility of police cruelty or atrocity, From the above cases, it is evident that any form of torture or cruel, inhuman or degrading treatments offensive to human dignity and constitutes an inroad into the right to life, and, therefore, prohibitive of Article 21 of the Constitution.' This approach of the Supreme Court is also in consonance with Article 5 of the Universal Declaration of Human Rights, Article 7 of the International Covenant of Civil and Political Rights and Declaration on the Protection of all persons from Being Subjected to Torture and other Cruel, Inhuman or Degrading Treatment of Punishment.

Khatri v. State of Bihar popularly known as *Bhagalpur Blinding* case, at one point of time even shocked the entire nation, This case depicts the extent to which police can go in committing atrocities on persons under its custody. In this case the Supreme Court considered the question of granting compensation to the victims of police atrocities and answered it in affirmative saying that if it were not so, Article 21 of the Constitution would be reduced to a nullity, "a mere rope of sand". Belatedly though, justice has finally caught up with the perpetrators of the blinding in Bhagalpur. The three police officials who were involved in the shocking incident of blinding of the undertrials, were finally convicted for taking the law into their hands.

From *Rudul Sah v. State of Bihar* to *PUDR v. State of Bihar*, the Apex Court has brought about revolutionary breakthrough in the "human rights jurisprudence" by evolving the principle that monetary compensation has to be paid to the victim of police atrocities. The Court has ruled that the State must repair the damage done by its officers by paying compensation to the victim and it may have recourse against the guilty officials.

A custodial death is perhaps one of the worst crimes in a civilized society governed by the rule of law. Custodial death as a result of police atrocities is the extreme form of police cruelty and the Courts in India have taken very serious view of such deaths.

In *SAHELI, a Women's Resources Centre v. Cominr. of Police, Delhi,* a child of 9 years died because of beating and assault by police officer. The Supreme Court held that the State is liable to pay compensation in case of police atrocities and accordingly it directed the government *to pay Rs. 75000 as* compensation to the mother of victim. The Court further observed that the Delhi Administration may take appropriate steps for recovery of the amount paid *as* compensation or part thereof from the officers who *will* he found responsible for such atrocities."

Nilabati Behera v. State of Orissa is yet another case of custodial death where the deceased was taken in police custody and next day his body was found on railway track with multiple injuries. The Supreme Court once again reiterated that in case of violation of fundamental rights by State's instrumentalities or servants. Court call direct the Slate to pay compensation to victim or his heir by way of 'monetary amends' and redressal.

The principle of "Sovereign immunity" shall be inapplicable in such cases. Having regard to the age and income of the deceased, the State was directed in this case to pay Rs. 1,50,000 as compensation to the deceased's mother. The Court further held that other liabilities of the respondents or any other person for custodial death remain unaffected. In other words, compensation in civil law or criminal law can still be claimed in addition to this. The Court clarified that "public law proceedings" are different from "private law proceedings" and the award of compensation in proceedings for the enforcement of fundamental right under

Articles 32 and 226 of the Constitution is a remedy available in public law. It was rightly observed:

> The Court is not helpless and the wide powers given to the Supreme Court by Article 32, which itself is a fundamental right, imposes a constitutional obligation on the Court to forge such new tools, which may be necessary for doing complete justice and enforcing the fundamental rights guaranteed in the Constitution, which enable the award of monetary compensation in appropriate cases..

To support the above observation, the Court rightly referred to Article 9(5) of the International Covenant on Civil and Political Rights, 1966 and held that the said provision indicates that an enforceable right to compensation is not alien to the concept of a guaranteed right.

Dr. A.S. Anand, J., while delivering a separate but concurring judgement in this case pointed out in sonorous terms that convicts, prisoners and undertrials also have the right under Article 21 of the Constitution and the State has strict duty to ensure that a person in custody of police is not deprived of his right except in accordance with law.

In *Pratul Kumar Sinha v. State of Bihar,* police atrocities lead to the death, of three young persons. One of them was bachelor while the other two were married and left behind their young widows. The Court issued directions for their ex-gratia payment of Rs. 25000 to the families of the deceased. The Court further held that if the State Government so desires it would be free to take such action as it considers necessary to recover this amount from the officers.

Whenever tiny case of human rights violation as a result of police atrocities has been brought before the Court, it has always taken a serious note of it and directed to make either judicial enquiry into the allegations of police atrocities or directed the Central Bureau of Investigation (CBI) to conduct an enquiry independently so as to fix the responsibility for violation of human rights.

In *Afzal v. State of Haryana, habeas corpus* petition was filed for the release of two children alleged to have been taken away by some police officials, and not produced before any magistrate. The arrest and detention of children was denied by the police. However, the report of Director General of Police and affidavit of S.P. revealed that the said children had been taken away by some police officials from their residence. The Court, in order to ascertain the truth of the whole case and role played by each of the respondent, directed the District Judge to conduct a detailed enquiry into the matter.

Inder Singh v. State of Punjab," is yet another case of human rights violation due to police atrocities. In this case seven persons ranging in age from 85 to 14 years were abducted by senior police officer (DSP) and sundry policemen used official machinery for this purpose. The State police acted leisurely and in most irresponsible manner in the whole case. The Supreme Court directed that the enquiry shall be conducted personally by the Director of the Central Bureau of Investigation (CBI).

The investigation was to cover, *inter* alia, the circumstances of abduction of the said seven persons; their present whereabouts or the date and circumstances of their liquidation and whether there has been an attempt to cover up the misdoings of police officers and policemen involved in the abduction of the said seven persons and their subsequent incarceration or liquidation. The court also made it clear that it shall be free to make such orders as are deemed necessary when the report of the Director, CBI is received, including the orders for payment of compensation by the respondents to the next of kin of the said seven persons.

Arvinder Singh Bagga v. State of U.P. is also a case of police atrocities where police officers were guilty of illegal arrest and torture in police station. They subjected a married woman to physical, mental and psychological torture calculated to create fright to make her submit to the demands of the police and abandon her legal marriage. Her husband and family members were also tortured. The Court took serious note of the human rights violation and directed the State to launch prosecution against the police officials concerned and directed to pay compensation of Rs. 10,000 to the victim woman and her husband and Rs. 5000 to each of the other victims. The Court further held that upon such payment it will be open to the state to recover personally the amount of compensation from the police officers concerned.

It is submitted that it would have been better if the Supreme Court had not left it open on the State government to recover the amount of compensation from guilty officials but directed to recover from them. However, the new concept of "personal liability" of the police officials, committing police atrocities leading to human rights violation, depicts the judicial wisdom in such cases and is a welcoming feature of the Indian judiciary. This will definitely have some deterrent effect on the police officials committing police atrocities and violating human rights.

As is evident from the Report of the National Police Commission, nearly 60% of the arrests by the police are either unnecessary or unjustified. And an analysis of above mentioned cases show that the Court has been receiving complaints about human rights violation because of indiscriminate arrests. For the effective enforcement of fundamental rights enshrined in Articles 21 and 22 of the Constitution of India and for protecting the human rights violation due to police atrocities, the Supreme Court has laid down following requirements:

1. An arrested person being held in custody is entitled, if he so requests to have one friend, relative or other person who is known to him or likely to take an interest in his welfare told as far as is practicable that he has been arrested and where he is being detained.
2. The police officer shall inform the arrested person when he is brought to the police station of this right.
3. An entry shall be required to be made in the diary as to who was informed of the arrest.

It shall be the duty of the Magistrate before whom the arrested person is produced, to satisfy himself that these requirements have been complied with.

The commitment of judiciary to protect the human rights violation due to police atrocities is evident when it observed that in cases of police brutality and atrocities committed in utter disregard and in all breaches of humanitarian law and universal human rights as well as in total negation of the Constitutional guarantees and human decency the Supreme Court is committed to uphold human rights even as a part of long-standing heritage and as enshrined in our Constitutional law.

This perspective needs to be kept in view by every law enforcing authority because the recognition of the inherent dignity and of the equal and inalienable rights of the citizen is the foundation of freedom, justice and peace in the world. If the human rights are outraged, then the Court should set its face against such violation of human rights by exercising its majestic judicial authority.

7

Measures for Curbing Torture

"A man of a right spirit is not a man of narrow and private views, but is greatly interested and concerned for the good of the community to which he belongs, and particularly of the city or village in which he resides, and for the true welfare of the society of which he is a mem-ber."

—*Jonathan Edwards*

Elimination of Torture

Torture is 'severe pain or suffering, whether physical or mental, inflicted by, or at the instigation of, a public official on a person, for such purposes as obtaining from him, or a third person, information or confession, punishing him for an act he has committed or is suspected of having committed or intimidating him or other persons for the same purpose. Torture has been in practice for centuries and has debased human conduct. It degrades and affects the dignity of person. All international instruments on human rights prohibit torture.

The Universal, Declaration of Human Rights in Article 5 states: "No one shall be Subjected to torture, or to Cruel, inhuman or degrading punishment."

The International Covenant on Civil and Political Rights

in Article 7 states: No' one shall be Subjected to torture or to cruel, inhuman or degrading treatment or punishment. In particular, no one shall be subjected, without his free consent, to medical or scientific experimentation.

The Constitution of India has no special provisions on the subject. However, the Supreme Court has drawn this protection against torture, cruel and unusual punishment from a combined reading of Articles 14, 19 and 26.

The Indian Penal Code, in Section 348, punishes wrongful confinement of a person to extort confession or compel restoration of property. Similarly, Section 330 regards the act of voluntarily causing hurt to extort confession or compel restoration of property as a punishable offence. In Section 362(2)(a), minimum punishment has been laid down for rape occurring in police custody.

To preserve human dignity, to ensure that the basic freedoms proclaimed in the Charter of United Nations are available and to promote universal respect for and the observance of human rights and fundamental freedoms, a Convention against Torture and Other Cruel or Inhuman or Degrading Treatment or Punishment was adopted by UN General Assembly on December 10,1984.

The Government of India has ratified this convention and the National Human Rights Commission has started a concerted drive to remove this evil from law enforcement and security forces.

Torture often takes place when security forces deal with suspected lawless elements to ferret out tactical information. These ire prohibited by the force's own regulations. Torture can be eliminated only when senior supervisory offices keep a close control over their subordinates while they handle people in custody and by constantly training them to adopt legal and human rights standards.

Public Fair and Speedy Trial

A citizen charged with a criminal Offence is presumed to be innocent till the charges against him are proved in a court of law beyond reasonable doubt. Thus, the, proceedings in a court, known as trial, is very important for him as it is at this forum where his innocence is being proved or disproved. The criminal justice process is initiated is soon as information about the commission of an offence is received and a case is registered and FIR issued. From this time onwards, till the investigation ferrets out the truth and a charge is laid before a court, the accused person has many basic rights. When the court actually starts proceeding to enquire into the charge, the trial process begins. There are many basic human rights assured to persons facing the trial to ensure justice is done to them, These are contained in human rights instruments and national laws:

Universal Declaration of Rights

Article 10 reads: Everyone is entitled to full equality to a fair and public hearing by an independent and impartial tribunal, in the determination of the rights and obligation and of any criminal charge against him".

International Covenant on Civil and Political Rights

Article 14(3) says: In the determination of any criminal charges against him, every one shall be entitled to the following minimum guarantees, in full equality:

(a) To be informed promptly and in detail in a language which he understands, of the nature and cause of his charge against him;

(b) To have adequate time and facilities for the preparation of his defence and to communicate with counsel of his own choosing;

(c) To be tried without undue delay;

(d) To be tried in his presence, and to defend himself in person or through legal assistance of his own choosing : to be informed, if he does not have legal assistance, of this right, and to have legal assistance assigned to him, in any case where the interests of justice so require, and without payment by him in any such case, if he does not have sufficient means to pay for it;

(e) To examine, or have examined, the witnesses against him and to obtain the attendance and examination of witnesses on his behalf under the same conditions as witnesses against him;

(f) To have the free assistance of an interpreter if he cannot understand or speak the language used in court; and

(g) Not to be compelled to testify against himself or to confess guilt.

Constitution of India in Article 21 says: No person shall be deprived of his life or persona] liberty except according to procedures established by law.

Procedures established by law or the due process as applied in India, requires that the trial Should:

(a) Give notice of hearing to the accused;

(b) Give accused an opportunity to be heard in defence;

(c) The hearing should be by an impartial tribunal; and

(d) 'Reasonable' restrictions can be placed on enjoyment of the rights of procedures.

The Supreme Court of India, through many decisions, has now made a compact set of rights accessible to an accused. They are:

(1) *Fair Hearing:* This right starts as soon as the magistrate takes the Charge on his file and invokes the provisions of section 202 Cr.P.C.

(2) *Notices:* The accused is entitled to have a notice of the hearing under section 204 Cr.P.C,

(3) *Open Trial:* Under section 327 Cr.P.C., the trial should be open and public. However, in cases of rape and sensitive national security matters, the court has a right to bar access to public.

(4) *Speedy Trial:* This right has been given as an extension of the concept of fairness enunciated in Article 21, The Supreme Court has extended this to pre-trial processes including investigation.

The accused can get relief through the medium of 'writs'. The right to a speedy trial is embodied in Section 309 of the Code of Criminal Procedure.

(5) *Right to an Interpreter:* This duty is cast on the court to ensure that the accused understands the proceedings and if necessary, the court can arrange for an interpreter. This is provided for in Section 279 of the Criminal Procedure Code, As a further safeguard, Section 318 of the Cr.P.C. stipulates where it appears that the accused has not understood the proceedings and the case ends in conviction, the matter should be placed before the High Court for orders.

(6) *Right to proper defence:* Constitution of India in Article 22(1) says -'No person who is arrested shall be

detained in custody without being informed, as soon as may be, of the grounds for such arrest nor shall he be denied the right to consult, and to be defended by a legal practitioner of his choice.

This right commences from the moment of arrest and extend throughout the trial, even if released on bail.

If the accused is poor, he is entitled to legal assistance at State' cost. This is provided for by Article 39(A) of the Constitution of India, Section 304(1) of the Code of Criminal Procedure and Legal Services Authorities Act of 1987.

(7) *Right to the opportunity to make a proper and full defence:* The accused has the right to get free copies of Police. Report, FIR, Confession, Statements of witnesses under Section 207,208 and 238 of Criminal Procedure Code. In all appealable cases, he should get a free certified copy of the judgement under Section 363 of the Cr.P.C.

All the witnesses against him - the prosecution witnesses are to be examined in his presence and he can cross-examine them. He can also get all the witnesses to speak on his behalf summoned by the Court and examined. The court however has a right not to summon all, as per Cr.P.C. 233(2) and 243(2), it is of the opinion that, they are not relevant and are being summoned as a dilatory tactics while the accused can not be examined to prove the guilt against him, he can offer himself as a witness to produce his defence. But any thing said in the nature of confession can not be admitted against him. He can only be called as a witness, when he makes a request for it.

(8) *Final opportunity:* After hearing both the sides and before pronouncing an order of punishment, the

court has to give an opportunity to the accused to make a representation against the same.

(9) *Right to Appeal:* The accused has a right to appeal against his conviction at higher judicial forums. All assistance and help should be given to him if he is a prisoner.

It will be seen that the Indian judicial and legal systems are very progressive in this area, and all the international standards were present in operation in spirit long before they came into vogue through covenants.

10. *Police to co-operate* : While it is the duty of the court to ensure that all these rights are available to the accused, the magistrate often needs the assistance of the police to provide copies of the statements of prosecution witnesses, serve summons, produce witnesses for examination etc. Police should willingly and readily co-operate with the courts to ensure that the accused get all their basic rights.

Methods of Combating Torture

Torture is a particularly serious violation of human rights and, as such, is strictly condemned by international law and, in particular, by the Universal Declaration of Human Rights, article 5, which states that "No one shall be subjected to torture or to cruel, inhuman or degrading treatment or punishment".

To ensure adequate protection for all persons against such abuses, the United Nations has sought for many years to develop universally applicable standards. The Convention against Torture and Other Cruel, Inhuman or Degrading Treatment or Punishment, which was adopted by the General Assembly of the United Nations on 10 December 1984, and many other relevant conventions, declarations and resolutions adopted by the international community, clearly state that there may be no exception to the prohibition against torture. The United Nations nevertheless notes that torture continues to be practised in a number of countries, To assist the many victims of torture, the General Assembly set up the United Nations Voluntary Fund for Victims of Torture in 1981. The establishment of the Fund was in no way intended to signify implicit acceptance of torture, The complete eradication of torture continues to be a major priority of the United Nations.

The use of torture and cruel, inhuman or degrading treatment is one of the very first issues that was dealt with at length and in depth by the United Nations a few years after its establishment, Over the years, the United Nations has sought in many ways to ensure adequate protection for all against torture and other cruel, inhuman or degrading treatment or punishment. It has adopted universal standards of protection applicable to everyone and embodied them in international declarations and conventions. It has also adopted particular standards applicable to persons deprived of their liberty, whether accused or convicted of a crime.

It has outlawed particular forms of treatment and punishment, has initiated studies leading to the preparation of a draft code of conduct for law enforcement officials and of a draft code of medical ethics. In addition, it has strengthened and reaffirmed the Standard Minimum Rules for the Treatment of Prisoners, which have provided some measure of protection to incarcerated persons since their formulation in 1955 and which have influenced the legislation of many countries.

Abolition of Corporal Punishment in Trust Territories

In 1949, the Trusteeship Council, in the report covering

its fourth and fifth sessions, recommended that corporal punishment should be abolished immediately in certain territories under colonial administration, In support of that recommendation, the General Assembly itself recommended, in resolution 440 (V) of 2 December 1950, that "measures be taken to bring about the complete abolition of corporal punishment in all Trust Territories where it still existed" and requested the administering authorities to report on the matter. Two years later, the General Assembly reviewed the reports which it had received and which showed that measures had been taken to reduce the number of offences in respect of which corporal punishment was applied.

Standard Minimum Rules for the Treatment of Prisoners

In 1955, the First United Nations Congress on the Prevention of Crime and the Treatment of Offenders adopted the Standard Minimum Rules for the Treatment of Prisoners prepared by an Advisory Committee of Experts established in accordance with the plan set out by the Secretary-General and approved by General Assembly resolution 415 (V) of 1 December 1950.

The purpose of the Standard Minimum Rules for the Treatment of Prisoners is not to describe in detail a model system of penal institutions, but, on the basis of the general consensus of contemporary thought and the essential elements of the most adequate systems of today, to set out what is generally accepted as being good principle and practice in the treatment of prisoners and the management of institutions. One of the Standard Minimum Rules (rule 31) provides that corporal punishment, punishment by placing in a dark cell, and all cruel, inhuman or degrading punishment shall be completely prohibited as punishments for disciplinary offences.

The General Assembly, in resolution 2858 (XXVI) of 20

December 1971, drew the attention of Member States to the Standard Minimum Rules and recommended that they should be effectively implemented in the administration of penal and correctional institutions. It also invited them to consider incorporating the Standard Minimum Rules in their national legislation.

Protection against Arbitrary Arrest and Detention

Draft principles on freedom from arbitrary arrest and detention were prepared at the request of the United Nations Commission on Human Rights (resolution 2 (XVII) of 14 March 1961) by a Committee composed of four member States of the Commission. With regard to the treatment of arrested or detained persons, article 24 of the draft principles stipulates that:

> No arrested or detained person shall be subjected to physical or mental compulsion, torture, violence, threats or inducements of any kind, deceit, trickery, misleading suggestions, protracted questioning, hypnosis, administration of drugs or any other means which tend to impair or weaken his freedom of action or decision, his memory or his judgement. Any statement which he may be induced into making through any of the above prohibited methods, as well as any evidence obtained as a result thereof, shall not be admissible in evidence against him in any proceedings ...

In decision 37/427 of 16 December 1982, the General Assembly decided that an open-ended working group of its Sixth Committee (legal questions) would be established at the outset of the thirty-eighth session with a view to expediting the finalization of the draft principles. As adopted in November 1987 by the Working Group, the draft body of principles for the protection of all persons under any form of detention or imprisonment includes a total of 39 principles preceded by definitions of terms such as "detention", "arrest", "detainee", "prisoner" and "judicial or other authority.

Principle 1 stipulates that,

> All persons under any form of detention or imprisonment shall be treated with humanity and with respect for the inherent dignity of the human person.

Principle 7 provides that:

> States shall prohibit by law any act contrary to the rights and duties contained in these Principles, make any act subject to appropriate sanctions and conduct impartial investigations upon complaints.

Declaration on Protection from Torture

The Declaration on Protection of All Persons from Being Subjected, to Torture and Other Cruel, Inhuman or Degrading Treatment or Punishment was adopted by the General Assembly in its resolution 3452 (XXX) of 9 December 1975. The Declaration contains 12 articles, the first of which defines the term "torture" as:

> any act by which severe pain or suffering, whether physical or mental, is intentionally inflicted by or at the instigation of a public official on a person for such purposes as obtaining from him or a third person information or confession, punishing him for an act he has committed or is suspected of having committed, or intimidating him or other persons.

Code of Conduct for Law Enforcement Officials

In resolution 34/169 of 17 December 1979, the General Assembly adopted a Code of Conduct for Law Enforcement Officials and transmitted it to governments with the recommendation that favourable consideration should be given to its use within the framework of national legislation or practice as a body of principles for observance by law enforcement officials. Article 5 of the Code reads as follows:

> No law enforcement official may inflict, instigate or tolerate any act of torture or other cruel, inhuman or degrading treatment or punishment, nor may any law enforcement official invoke superior orders or exceptional circumstances such as a state of war or threat of war, a threat to national security, internal political instability or any other public emergency as a justification of torture or other cruel, inhuman or degrading treatment or punishment.

Principles of Medical Ethics

In resolution 37/194 of 18 December 1982, the General Assembly adopted the Principles of Medical Ethics relevant to the role of health personnel, particularly physicians, in the protection of prisoners and detainees against torture and other cruel, inhuman or degrading treatment or punishment.

Principle 1 of the Principles of Medical Ethics provides that:

> Health personnel, particularly physicians, charged with the medical care of prisoners and detainees, have a duty to provide them with protection of their physical and mental health and treatment of disease of the same quality and standard as is afforded to those who are not imprisoned or detained,

Principle. 2 states that:

> It is a gross contravention of medical ethics, as well as an offence under applicable international instruments, for health personnel, particularly physicians, to engage, actively or passively, in acts which constitute participation in, complicity in,

incitement to or attempts to commit torture or other cruel, inhuman or degrading treatment or punishment

Convention against Torture

The Convention against Torture and Other Cruel, Inhuman or Degrading Treatment or Punishment was adopted by the United Nations General Assembly on 10 December 1984. It consists of 33 articles which became effective as of 26 June 1987.

(a) Features of the Convention

The Convention against Torture and Other Cruel, Inhuman or Degrading Treatment or Punishment not only specifies that the States Parties will outlaw torture in their national legislation, but also notes explicitly that no order from a superior or exceptional circumstance may be invoked as a justification of torture. The Convention also introduces two new elements of particular significance to efforts by the United Nations to combat torture. The first is that, henceforth a torturer may be prosecuted wherever he is to be found in the territory of any State Party to the Convention, since the Convention specifies that persons alleged to have committed acts of torture may be tried in any State Party or that they may be extradited so that they may be tried in the State Party where they committed their crimes.

The second new element is that the Convention contains a provision which allows for an international inquiry if there is reliable information indicating that torture is being systematically practised in the territory of a State Party to the Convention, Such an inquiry may include a visit to the State Party concerned, with its agreement.

The States Parties to the Convention also pledge to take effective legislative, administrative, judicial or other measures to prevent acts of torture in any territory under their jurisdiction. No exceptional circumstances whatsoever, whether a state of war, internal political instability or any other public emergency, may be invoked as a justification of torture.

Under the Convention, no State Party may expel, return or extradite a person to another State where there are substantial grounds for believing that he would be in danger of being subjected to torture.

The States Parties agree to afford one another the greatest measure of assistance in connection with criminal proceedings brought forward in respect of acts of torture, and to ensure that education and information regarding the prohibition against torture are fully included in the training of law enforcement personnel, civil or military, medical personnel, public officials and other persons who may be involved in the custody, interrogation or treatment of any individual subjected to any form of arrest, detention or imprisonment.

The States Parties also undertake to ensure in their legal systems that the victims of acts of torture obtain redress and have an enforceable right to fair and adequate compensation, including the means for as full rehabilitation as possible.

(b) Implementation of the Convention

The implementation of the Convention is monitored by the United Nations Committee against Torture, which consists of 10 experts of high moral standing and recognized competence in the field of human rights. Under article 19 of the Convention, the States Parties submit to the Committee, through the Secretary-General of the United Nations, reports on the measures they have taken under the Convention. Each report is considered by the Committee, which may make general comments and include such information in its annual report to the States Parties and to the General Assembly.

Under article 20 of the Convention, if the Committee receives reliable information which appears to contain well-founded indications that torture is being systematically practised in the territory of a State Party, the Committee invites that State Party to co-operate in the examination of the information and, to this end, to submit observations with regard to the information concerned, The Committee may, if it decides that this action is warranted, designate one or more of its members to make a confidential inquiry and to report to the Committee urgently In agreement with that State Party, such an inquiry may include a visit to its territory.

After examining the findings of its member or members submitted to it, the Committee transmits these findings to the State Party concerned together with any comments or suggestions which seem appropriate in view of the situation.

All the proceedings of the Committee are confidential and, at all stages of the proceedings, the co-operation of the State Party is sought. After such proceedings have been completed, the Committee may, after consultations with the State Party concerned, decide to include a summary account of the results of the proceedings in its annual report to the other States Parties and to the General Assembly of the United Nations.

The Committee against Torture

The Committee against Torture was established pursuant to article 17 of the Convention. It consists of 10 experts elected by the States Parties by secret ballot. The members of the Committee are elected for four years and are eligible for re-election. The main function of the Committee against Torture is to ensure that the Convention against Torture and Other Cruel, Inhuman or Degrading Treatment or Punishment is observed and implemented. The present Committee was set up on 26 November 1987 at the initial meeting in Geneva of the States Parties to the Convention.

The expenses incurred in connection with the Committee's activities are borne by the States Parties to the Convention. At their initial meeting, the States Parties decided that they would share expenses in proportion to their contributions to the budget of the United Nations, but that no single State's share should be more than 25 per cent of total expenses. The initial meeting of the members of the Committee against Torture was held in Geneva, Switzerland, in April 1988. At that meeting, the Committee adopted its rules of procedure, defined its working methods in accordance with the provisions of the Convention under which it had been set up and considered procedural matters. It also decided to hold two sessions in 1989. Under rule 62 of its rules of procedure, the Committee may invite specialized agencies, United Nations bodies concerned, regional intergovernmental organizations and non-governmental organizations in consultative status with the Economic and Social Council to submit to it information, documentation and written statements, relevant to the Committee's activities under the Convention.

The 10 members elected to the Committee serve in their personal capacity and took office on 1 January 1988. They include: Mr. Alfredo R.A. Bengzon (Philippines), Mr. Peter Thomas Burns (Canada), Ms. Christine Chanet (France), Mr. Socorro D - az Palacios (Mexico), Mr. Alexis Dipanda Mouelle (Cameroon), Mr. Ricardo Gil Lavedra (Argentina), Mr. Yuri A. Khitrin (USSR), Mr. Dimitar Nikolov Mikhailov (Bulgaria), Mr. Bent Sorensen (Denmark) and Mr. Joseph Voyame (Switzerland).

As half the Committee is replaced every two years, five of the 10 experts, whose names were drawn by lot at the initial meeting of the States Parties to the Convention on 26 November 1987, will complete their term at the end of 1989 instead of 1991

Special Rapporteur on Torture

In addition to the drafting of the text of the Convention, the United Nations Commission on Human Rights, in resolution 1985/33, appointed a special rapporteur to examine questions relevant to torture, requesting him to seek and receive credible and reliable information on such questions and to respond to that information without delay.

While the terms of reference of the Committee against Torture give it a quasi-legal function, the mandate of the Special Rapporteur on questions relevant to torture is entirely different. He is required to report to the Commission, which is composed of government representatives, on the phenomenon of torture in general. To this end, the Special Rapporteur establishes contact with governments and asks them for information on the legislative and administrative measures taken to prevent torture and to remedy its consequences whenever it occurs.

The Special Rapporteur is also expected to respond effectively to the credible and reliable information that comes before him. This provision of the Special Rapporteur's mandate has led to the urgent action procedure, which considerably increases the effectiveness of his activities.

Unlike that of the Committee, the Special Rapporteur's task is not confined to the States Parties to the Convention against Torture; it extends to all Member States of the United Nations and to all States with observer status. He corresponds with governments, requesting them to inform him of the measures they have taken or plan to take to prevent or combat torture. He also receives requests for urgent action, which he brings to the attention of the governments concerned in order to ensure protection of the individual's right to physical and mental integrity. In addition, he holds consultations with government representatives who express the wish to meet with him and, in accordance with his mandate, makes "on site consultation" visits to some parts of the world.

For his future activities, the Special Rapporteur recommended to the most recent session of the Commission on Human Rights, held in Geneva in early 1988, that:

- Detention incommunicado should be declared illegal;
- Any person who is arrested should be brought without delay before a competent judge, who should rule immediately on the lawfulness of his arrest and authorize him to see a lawyer;
- Any person arrested should undergo a medical examination;
- Any detainee who dies should be autopsied in the presence of a representative of his family-, and, External experts should regularly inspect places of detention.

8

Standards and Actions

"Instead of saying that man is the creature of circumstance, it would be nearer the mark to say that man is the architect of circumstance. It is character which builds an existence out of circumstance. From the same materials one man builds palaces, another hovels; one warehouses, another villas; bricks and mortar are mortar and bricks until the architect can make them something else."

—*Thomas Carlyle*

National Standards

Use of torture by the police for the purpose or extracting confession from the suspected offender is a routine affair in India. The investigation procedure remains as outmoded as it was during the pro-Independence days when Justice Sir Walsh of the Allahabad High Court, had occasion to comment: "Whereas the English detective begins with his available witnesses, and works his way up to the discovery of truth, the Indian sub-inspector begins with the accused and from him works his way tip to witnesses."

The most common torture method is severe beating. Sometimes the victim is hung upside down and given electric shock. We have also reports of crushing of suspected offenders, their burning, their stabbing with sharp instruments and forcing of objects like chilli or thick sticks into their rectum by the police. Sexual mutilation has also been reported. Rape, common form of torture, is very often used by the police and the security forces to deter the opposition and also as a means of indirectly punishing the men from a particular village or area.

A few recent event in which policemen were involved shows the extent to which police violence and high-handedness may extend. In a sensational Baghpat episode a married woman of a respectable family was alleged to have been made to walk nude through the town after her husband and another man were killed by the policemen just because the deceased had protested to the teasing of the woman by a Police officer. The Bhagalpur police in Bihar earned worldwide notoriety when it came to light that they had been blinding a number of undertrial persons by the 'acid treatment'. Besides, there are reports of fake police encounters involving cold-blooded murder of suspected offenders in police custody, The victims of police torture are mainly poorest and most vulnerable groups of people such as *Dalits'* and 'Adivasis.'

"Torture" has not been defined in the Constitution or in other penal laws. "Torture" of a human being by another human being is essentially oil instrument to impose the will of the "strong" over the it weak" by suffering. The word torture today has become synonymous with the darker, side of human civilisation.

The Supreme Court in D.K. Basu further quoting Adriana P. Bartow slated:

> "Torture is a wound in the soul so painful that sometimes you can almost touch it, but it is also so intangible that there is not way to heal it. Torture is

anguish squeeing in your chest, cold as ice and heavy as a stone, paralysing as sleep and dark as the abyss. Torture is despair and fear and rage and hate. It is a desire to kill and destroy including yourself."

The 1975 U.N. Declaration on the Protection of All Persons from Torture and other Cruel and Inhuman or Degrading Treatment or Punishment defines 'torture' as:

> "...any act by which severe pain or suffering, whether physical or mental, is intentionally inflicted by or at the instigation of a public official on a person for such purpose as obtaining from him or the third person information or confession punishing him for an act he was committed or is suspected of having committed or intimidating him or other persons..."

The Convention against Torture adopted by the General Assembly on 10 December 1984 defines torture as follows:

> "For the purposes of this Convention, the term "torture" means any act by which severe pain or suffering whether physical or mental, is intentionally inflicted on a person for such purposes as obtaining from him or a third person information or a confession, punishing him for all act he or a third person has committed or intimidating or coercing him or a third person, or for any reason based oil discrimination of any kind, when such pain or suffering is inflicted by or at the instigation of or with the consen or acquiescence of a public official or other person acting in the official capacity. It does not include pain or suffering arising only from inherent in or incidental to lawful sanctions."

India has not so far acceded to the Convention Against Torture but the Indian laws provide certain measures of protection to pre-trial detainees from police torture. Apart from protections provided in Articles 19, 20, 21, 22, 32 and

226 of the Constitution, safeguards against police torture are provided ill the criminal law and procedure of the land. Various Police and Prison Acts and Manuals also contain certain rules against torture.

Protection Under General Criminal

It is good to note in this connection that torture has been made a punishable offence under Sections 220, 330 and 331 of the Indian Penal Code, Section 220 provides for punishment to an officer or authority the detains or a keep a person in confinement with a corrupt or malicious motive. Voluntarily causing hurt to extort confession or information is an offence under Section 330 punishable with seven years imprisonment and fine and 10 years imprisonment for causing grievous hurt under Section 331.

Under Section 54 of the Code of Criminal Procedure, the accused person if brought before a Magistrate can request a medical examination. This provisions runs as follows:

> "When a person who is arrested, whether on a charge or otherwise, alleges, at the time when he is produced before a Magistrate or at any time during the period of his detention in custody that the examination of his body will afford evidence which will disprove the commission by him of any offence or which will establish the commission by any other person of any offence against his body, the Magistrate shall, if requested by the arrested person so to do direct the examination of the body of such person by a registered medical practitioner unless the Magistrate considers that the request is made for the purpose of vexatious delay or for defeating the ends of justice,"

The object of this Section is to confer on the arrested person the right to have his medical examination done. It was field in *D.J. Vaghela v. Kantibhai Jethabhai* that the Magistrate owes a duty to inform the arrested person about his right to get himself examined in case he has complaints of physical torture or maltreatment in police custody. The supreme Court has cautioned the lower courts not to adopt a casual approach to custodial torture. In case the Magistrate considers the request of the accused to be vexations or for defeating the ends of justice, he may refuse it. It has been held in Mukesh Kumar V, State that the procedure adopted by the Magistrate to examine the body of the accused himself and then dismissing the application with his observation that they were seen in normal posture was wholly unwarranted and erroneous.

Protection Against self-Incrimination

As noted earlier, torture is used by police to extract a self-incriminating statement or a confession from the suspected offender. Article 20(3) of the Constitution provides ample safeguards against compulsion of self-incrimination. The privilege under this provision is available to a person accused of an offence. It prohibits the compulsion of the accused to give evidence against himself. Section 162 of the Criminal Procedure Code is another provision which seeks to protect persons suspected of crimes from police brutalities by imposing a general bar against the use of a statement made before the police except for the limited purpose set out in the proviso It is however permissible to use the statement for the limited purpose or contradicting a witness if there is an inconsistency between his statement made before the police and the subsequent testimony in event.

Inadmissibility of Custodial Confessions

Sections 24, 25, 26 and 27 of the Evidence Act are also meant to protect persons suspected of crimes from police atrocities and high-handedness. The effect of the first three provisions is inadmissibility of a confession made by an accused person to a police officer or made by him while in police custody in judicial proceedings. But whatever protection is afforded by these provisions to an accused person from police coercion is nullified by Section 27 of the Act. Section 27, a very potent source of police brutality, provides that the information furnished by an accused after his arrest to the investigating officer which leads to the discovery of articles is admissible in evidence. It does not in any way offend Article 20(3) or the Constitution, Explaining the rationale or Section 27 the Supreme Court, in State of U.P. v. *Deoman Upadhyaya* observed:

> "Section 27 is founded on the principle that even though *the* evidence relating to confessional or other statements made by a person, whilst he is in the custody of a police officer, is and therefore inadmissible, if the truth of the information given by him is assured by the discovery of a fact, it may he presumed to he untainted and is therefore declared provable in so far it distinctly relates to the fact thereby discovered."

Death due to torture in custody is murder under the Indian Penal Code for which the maximum punishment is death penalty., Section 29 of the Police Act. 1861 also lays down that torture in custody is a punishable offence." In addition, various Police Acts at the State level prescribe custodial torture and direct the station house officer (SHO) of police to keep the suspects safe from any physical assault while in the police custody."

Rulings and Directions of the Supreme Court

Although the Constltutlon does riot contain any specific provision against torture, the Supreme Court in a series of cases, has come down heavily on the police for its atrocities, hold torture or cruel, inhuman, or degrading treatment which trenches on human dignity as impermissible under the Constitution and gave certain directions to the police to improve the conditions of police-lockups and to minimise the possibility of police excesses on the suspected offenders". In *D.K. Basu v. State of W.B.* the Supreme Court observed that "custodial torture is naked violation of human dignity and degradation which destroys, to a very large extent, the individual personality. It is a calculated assault on human dignity and whenever human dignify is wounded civilisation takes a step backward-flag of humanity must on each such occasion fly half-mast."

All this notwithstanding torture and degrading treatment of suspect by the police continues as evident from some of the cases decided by the apex court. Thus in *Niranjan Singh"*, the court lamented that "the police instead of being the protector of law have become the engineer of terror and panic the people into fear." The highest court was again deeply disturbed by the diabolical recurrence of police torture resulting in a terrible scare in the minds of common citizens *in Raghubir Singh v. State of Haryana,* where the violence employed by the police to extract a confession resulted in the death of a person suspected of death. It observed:

> "(T)heir lives and liberty are under a new peril when the guardians of the law gore human rights to death. The vulnerability of human rights assumes a traumatic, torture sonic poignancy, the violent violation is perpetrated by the police arm of the State whose function is to protect the citizens and not to commit gruesome offences against them as has happened in this case. Police lock up, if reports in newspapers have a streak of credence, are becoming more and more awesome cells. This development is disastrous to our human rights awareness and humanist constitutional order."

The court hoped that, "the State, at the highest administrative and political levels", will organize special strategies to prevent and punish brutality by police methodology, "otherwise the credibility of the rule of law in our republic vis-a-vis the people of the country will deteriorate." In *Kishore Singh* severe strictures were passed by the Court against the police force for its gruesome act of torture. The court observed:

> Nothing is more cowardly and unconscionable than, person in police custody being beaten up and nothing inflicts a deeper wound on our constitutional culture than a State official running berserk regardless of human rights.

The court suggested the police to depend "its wits and not fists" and "culture and not oil torture" for their investigation. It advised the Government to "re-educate the police, to weed them out of their sadistic tendencies and inculcate in them the respect for human person and punish those responsible for custodial torture". The court hoped that the police cruelty would receive the serious attention of the Government otherwise "who will police the police'.

In *Nandini Satpathy v. P.L. Dani* the court held that, the right not to make self-incriminatory statements should be widely interpret to cover the pre-trial stage of police investigations. It criticised the police for calling women to police stations for investigation saying this constituted a violation of Section 160(1) of the Cr.P.C., which requires the police to interview males under 15 and women in the place where they reside.

In *Sheela Barse* the Supreme Court made following directions and suggestions to the State Government to prevent the recurrence of police torture. *First,* the State Government should prepare pamphlets in local languages describing the rights of arrested persons which should be placed in each police cell so as to enable all detainees in police custody to know their rights. Secondly, the police should inform the nearest Legal Aid Committee immediately of an arrest so that the committee might provide assistance at once at Government expense. Thirdly, the relatives of the arrested person should be immediately informed by the police. Fourthly, male detainees should be kept separate from female detainees and a female officer should be present during the interrogation of women detainees. Fifty City and Sessions Judges should make unannounced visits to police stations to check on the treatment of inmates. And finally, Magistrates before whom detainees appear must enquire whether they had complaints of police torture, and to inform all detainees that they have a right to a medical examination under Section 54 of Cr.P.C.

However, these sensible directives have not been implemented by the vast majority of officials, police and Magistrates. No wonder cases like that of *Ram Sagar Yadav* continue to take place. In the instant case a farmer was done to death in police custody because he made complaint against a police constable for demanding bribe. This case brings into sharp focus the reasons responsible for non-conviction of police officers or for their conviction for lesser offences. Although on the basis of proved facts the policeman could have been adjudged guilty of murder, the trial judge convicted him of culpable homicide not amounting to murder under the second part of Section 304 and awarded 7 years' rigorous imprisonment.

Later, the High court set aside both the conviction and the sentence. The Supreme Court affirmed the conviction and sentence but noted with regret that the trial judge did not find the policeman guilty or murder. The judgment throws light on the special difficulties involved with the proof of torture by the police personnel and recommends a change in the law of evidence to prevent the escape of the policemen guilty of custodial torture. The Court observed:

> "Before we close, we would like to impress upon the Government the need to amend the low appropriately so that policeman who commit atrocities on persons who are in their custody are not allowed to escape by reason of paucity or absence of evidence. Police Officers alone, and none else can give evidence as regards the circumstances in which a person in their custody comes to receive injuries while in their custody. Bound by ties of a kind of brotherhood, they often prefer to remain silent in such situations and when they choose to speak, they put their own gloss upon facts and pervert the truth. The result is that persons on whom atrocities are perpetrated by the police in the sanctum sanctorum of the police station, are left without any evidence to prove who the offenders are. The law as to burden of proof in such cases may be re-examined by legislature so that hand-maids of law and other do not use their authority and opportunities for oppressing the innocent citizens who look to them for protection".

Gauri Shankar Sharma v. State of U.P, is a typical case of a police officer trying to rescue his colleague by giving evidence favourable to the accused policeman. The High Court persuaded itself to believe that the police officer did not give false evidence since by doing so he would have risked losing his job, Consequently, the high Court set aside the conviction, under Section 304 Part II and some other provisions of the Indian Penal Code and Prevention of Corruption Act, of the Officer-in-Charge of the police station for fatal injuries inflicted to a person suspected of decoity. Restoring the conviction and sentence of 7 years by the trial court and rejecting the plea for substitution of imprisonment by fine, the Supreme Court rightly observed:

> "The offence is of a serious nature aggravated by the fact that it was committed by a person who is supposed to protect the Citizens and not misuse his uniform and authority to brutally assault them while *in* his custody Death in police custody must be seriously viewed for otherwise we will help take a stride in the direction of policeraj. It must be curbed with a heavy hand. The punishment should be such as would deter others from indulging in such behaviour. There can be no room-for leniency".

In DK Basu v, State of W.B. the Hon'ble Supreme Court made it clear that, Custodial violence, including torture and death in the lock-ups, strikes a blow at the rule of law, which demands that the powers of the executive should not only be derived from law but al so that the same should be limited by law. Custodial violence is a matter of concern. It is aggravated by the fact that it is committed by persons who are supposed to be the protectors of the citizens. It is committed under the shield of uniform and authority in the four walls of a police station or lock-up, the victim being totally helpless. The protection of an individual from torture and abuse by the police and other law-enforcing officers is a matter of deep concern in a free society.

Inquiry in the Cases of Custodial Deaths

Death caused by police torture in custody is most heinous offence committed by the police on the suspected offenders. For this reason there is a legally mandatory obligation of the State to order a magisterial inquiry in all cases of death in police custody. Section 176 of the Code of Criminal Procedure, 1973, reads:

1. When any person dies while in the custody of the police or when the case is of the nature referred to in clause (i) or clause (ii) of subsection (3) of Section 174 the nearest Magistrate empowered to hold inquests shall, and in any other case mentioned in sub-section (1) of Section 174, any Magistrate so empowered may hold an inquiry into the cause of death either instead of, or in addition to, the investigation held by the Police Officer; and if he does so, he shall have all the powers in conducting it which he would have in holding an inquiry into an offence.
2. The Magistrate holding such an inquiry shall record the evidence taken by him, in connection therewith in any manner hereinafter prescribed according to the circumstances of the case.
3. Whenever such Magistrate considers it expedient to make an examination of the dead body of any person who has been already interred, in order to discover the cause of his death, the Magistrate may cause the body to be disinterred and examined.
4. Where an inquiry is to be held under this Section, the Magistrate shall, wherever practicable, inform the relatives of the deceased whose names and addresses are known, and shall allow them to remain present at the inquiry.

Regrettably, such inquiries are often not held and whenever they are held their reports are often not accessible to the public. Such Inquiries can be hold either by an Executive Magistrate or by a Judicial Magistrate. In practice, most inquiries are conducted by Executive Magistrates, who have limited powers of investigation and must rely on evidence provided by the police. Moreover, they very often work under police pressure, For these reasons their inquiries are not commonly perceived as independent and impartial. Public opinion often demands instead a judicial inquiry because such inquiry is widely believed to be the most authoritative, independent and impartial type of investigation, In fact, high percentage of judicial inquiries have effectively established police culpability. However, officials tend to avoid judicial inquiries describing them as time consuming and unnecessary what usually happens in practice in the name of magisterial inquiry has been-vividly depicted in the following editorial *of The* Statesmen of 4 August, 1989.

"The demand for a judicial probe is easily reconciled with the one by an Executive Magistrate. The dependants of the victim are soon left alone to make a statement before the inquiring Magistrate. The police and their henchmen remain at liberty to play tricks upon the family distraught by the loss. The political parties conveniently forget that the magistracy is another arm of the government that is only too found of working in tandem with the police. This phenomenon has been laid bare time and again and one never hears of the outcome of the protracted magisterial, inquiries into such cases. The guilty policeman are taken as a part of the official fraternity and invariably rejoin the force after spending a few months in oblivion".

In view of the fact that percentage of inquiries which disclosed actionable material is highest in the case of judicial inquiries, lower in magisterial inquiries and lowest in inquiries conducted by other agencies, the National Police Commission has rightly recommended that judicial inquiries should be mandatory and held in all cases of "alleged rape of a woman in police, custody" and "death or grievous hurt caused while in police custody", Unfortunately, this sensible recommendation has not been implemented as yet and judicial inquiries are exceptional held.

Right to Compensation of the Victims

The award of monetary compensation, as a claim in public law for contravention of human rights, guaranteed in the Constitution, is an acknowledged remedy for the enforcement and protection of such rights. The courts have the obligation to satisfy the social aspirations of the citizens because the courts and the law are for: the people and expected to respond to their aspirations. Award of compensation for established infringement of the indefeasible rights guaranteed under Article 21 of the Constitution is a remedy available in public law since the purpose of public law is not only to civilise public power but also to assure the citizens that they live under a legal system wherein their rights and interests shall be protected and preserved.

Successive Indian Governments have persistently resisted all attempts to establish the right to monetary compensation for wrongful actions by their agents and officers when discharging "sovereign functions". All this however, could not prevent the Supreme Court front recognizing the right to compensation of the victims of the official abuses.

In the 1981 Bhagalpur bindings case the Supreme Court held the State liable for acts of its servants even if they acted beyond their authority. In 1983 tile Supreme Court ruled that a person whose right to life and personal liberty has been violated by the State is entitled to compensation which can be awarded both in a *habeas corpus* petition and a civil suit for damages." Three years later the Supreme Court awarded compensation to Mr. Bhim Singh, a member of the Jammu and Kashmir State Legislative Assembly for his illegal arrest and detention. In awarding Bhim Singh Rs. 50,000 for the wrongful deprivation of his liberty, the Supreme Court said:

> "If the personal liberty of a Member of the Legislative Assembly is to be played with in this fashion, one can only wonder at what may happen to lesser mortals! Police officers who are custodians of the law and the order should have the greatest respect for the personal liberty of the citizen and should not flout the laws by stooping to such bizarre acts of lawlessness".

In 1989 the Supreme Court awarded Rs. 75,000 compensation to Mrs. Kamlesh Kumari whose nine-year-old son was beaten to death by Delhi police officers. This is first known judgment in which the Supreme Court explicitly ruled that the State is liable to pay compensation to the victims of police misconduct. Alhough a Sessions Court in Andhra Pradesh had dismissed a civil claim for damages on grounds of "sovereign immunity" the Andhra Pradesh High Court, on appeal, held the State directly liable for deaths in police and judicial custody. In granting damages in 1999 to Ramakrishna Reddy, whose father had been killed in jail by personal rivals, the Andhra Pradesh High Court held:

> "Where a citizen has been deprived of his life or liberty otherwise than in accordance with the procedure established by law, it is no answer to say that the said deprivation was brought about while the officials of the State were acting in discharge of the sovereign functions of the State".

The plea of sovereign immunity has no application in the police custodial death and it is no defence for the State to escape from its liability to pay compensation for contravention of fundamental rights. This view was taken by the Supreme Court. In Nilabati Behera v. State of Orissa. In this case the court while awarding Rs, 1.50,000 as compensation to the deceased mother made it clear that there can be no question of availability of the defence of sovereign immunity in case of constitutional remedy. The court further said that its powers under Article 32 are wide enough to enable it to award compensation in appropriate cases where this is the only mode of redress available for contravention of fundamental rights." Since then this view has been reiterated in a series of cases viz. *Nilabati Behera* to D.K. *Basu*.

In *People's Union for Democratic Rights v. Police Commissioner, Delhi Police Headquarter. A* labourer who was taken to the police station for doing some work, was severely beaten when he demanded wages. The Supreme Court held that the State was liable to pay as compensation Rs. 75,000 to the family of the deceased.

In *State of Maharashtra v. Ravikant Patil,"* the Bombay High Court hold that handcuffing and parading of the petitioner was unwarranted and violative of Article 21 and directed the Inspector of Police who was responsible for this to pay Rs. 10,000 by way of compensation.

In T.C. *Pathak v. State of U.P.* the Supreme Court directed the State Government to pay a sum of Rs. 10,000 to detenu by way of compensation for the denial of his constitutional right under Article 21 of the Constitution. The award of this compensation is independent of any remedy which the detenu may have in private law for damages against the persons responsible for his illegal detention and torture.

Torture, Custodial Death and Public Interest Litigation (PIL)

Unfortunately, the court rulings which protect the 'pre-trail detainees' rights remain the exception to the rule, Faced with the reality that the vast majority of the Indian population are unaware of their rights and lack the financial and other resources to exercise them, imaginative civil rights and judicial activists invented the concept of public interest litigation. This is a public redress system unique to India. It cuts through the usual lengthy and costly legal formalities by allowing the poorest victims of human rights abuses to approach the Supreme Court directly, or if the victim can not do so him or herself, through a *bona fide* organization or person. The Supreme Court has even acted on a simple letter or postcard written by a prisoner.

The Supreme Court's judgment in the *Sheela Barse* case resulted from a letter the journalist had written to the court complaining of custodial violence to which women were subjected in Bombay police stations.

However, public interest litigation is now less often used for a number of reasons. These include the inability of the Supreme Court to deal with such cases because of lack of resources, the disinclination or inability of many judges to hear them or give such cases priority and the small number of lawyers concerned to use the potential for effective human rights protection. Perhaps the most important reason, however, is the lack of official support.

Undoubtedly, the victims of police excesses have the opportunity to bring a civil suit for damages or to initiate a criminal complaint. However, civil claims involve such lengthy and costly procedures that very few use them and complaints against the police a rarely successful. In the case of *Ramakrishna Reddy* cited above," the Andhra Pradesh High Court dismissed civil claims as an ineffective means of redress: "A civil remedy is a case of chasing a mirage and criminal action is no solace".

Criminal action can also be taken against police excesses, but very few police officers are ever brought to trial and most of them escape conviction for the want of required degree of proof. Even in rare cases of conviction the police personnel are very often adjudged guilty for lesser offences than the one warranted by the actual facts. Whenever report of police fortune comes to light senior police, executive magistrate, doctors and state officials work in tandem to cover-up such crimes or shield the police officers from being brought to justice. The result is that the police personnel are generally not scared of any criminal action and the use of third degree method continues to flourish,

Inquiry by the National Human Rights Commission

There is also provision for inquiry into allegation of police torture by the National Human Rights Commission under the Protection of Human Rights Act, 1993 (Act, No. 10 of 1994). The Annual Report 1994-95 of the N.H.R.C. provides an analysis of the 1660 particularly grave cases admitted by the Commission for investigation/inquiry during the year under report, relating essentially to violence against the human person. According to this report 111 of these cases relate to death in police custody, 51 to death in judicial custody and 9 to death while in the custody of other State agencies (the Armed Forces or the Forest Department). It further states that 497 cases relate to allegations of Various forms of police excesses, including the use of torture or third-degree methods in interrogation, while 114 cases allege illegal detention." The Annual Report 1995-96 of the Commission also provides an analysis of the 4081 cases in which the Commission asked for further reports and inquiries.

The commission is doing commendable work to prevent the abuse of human rights by the police by closely monitoring cases of custodial torture, custodial death and rape, all over the country and asking the State Government to take corrective measures including stringent action against the aberrant staff. The result have been positive for the protection of human rights,. For instance, during the year 1995-96, criminal prosecutions have been launched against 22 police officers and recommended against 20 others. Further more, departmental proceedings have been initiated in 26 cases and 79 police personnel have been placed under suspension.

The National Human Rights Commission has urged all States and Union Territories to constitute State Human Rights Commissions and notify a court of sessions to be a Human Right's court in each district as envisaged by Sections 21 and 30 respectively of the Protection of Human Rights Act. 1993. Under the Indian federal system such as ours it is evident that a concrete responsibility must rest with individual states both to promote and protect human rights and to redress grievances. The decentralisation of the complaint disposal mechanism thus becomes a necessity, not least so as to provide a redressal mechanism that is readily accessible and inexpensive in terms of time and cost. States have, in addition, been urged to establish district-level Committees for effective and speedy redressal of complaints of human right's violations."

Reasons for the Use of Torture by the Police

Before we proceed to discuss the possible remedial measures, let us have a brief look at the predominant reasons for the use of torture by the police. The first and foremost reason is the negative public image of the police due to which they do not get requisite public support in their task or crime prevention and crime control. They are still seen to quote Justice Mulla's words, the largest single lawless group in the country. As a matter of fact the situation has not altered very much since Mr. Justice Straight made the following pessimistic observation about the police in 1884:

> These legislative Provisions leave no doubt -in my mind that the legislature had in view the malpractices of police officers in extorting confessions from accused person in order to gain credit by securing convictions and that those malpractices went to the length of positive torture: nor do I doubt that the legislature, in laying down such stringent rules, regards the evidence of public officers untrustworthy ....

It requires no vivid imagination to picture what too often takes place when two or three of these not very intellectual highly paid police officer are called away to a village to investigate a grave crime of which there no very clear traces. Naturally, it is much the easier way for them to begin by endeavouring to obtain a confession from the suspected person or persons instead of searching out the clues to the evidence from independent sources:

> ... I say it in no harsh sense of disparagement, but it is impossible not to feel that the average Indian policemen....is not likely to be over *nice* in the, methods he adopts to make a short cut to the elucidation of a difficult case by getting a suspected person to confess".

There are many reasons for bad police image as rightly observed by Justice O. Chinappa Reddy;

> "I think it is due to a combination of several circumstances. Occasional high-handed behaviour including acts of violence; occasional perjury; more important than the actual high-handedness and perjury an attitude of casualness and indifference in the exercise of high-handedness and the giving of perjured evidence; the corruption of a few; a general misunderstanding of the police procedure, method and work; a remainder of one's own acts of trespass and a general resentment of authority are several of the factors which contribute to a citizen's hostility towards a policemen".

Implementation of recommendations for police reform such as those proposed by the National Police Commission, would have improved the police image in the eyes of the general public but unfortunately those recommendations has been ignored by successive Central and State Governments POOR working conditions of the lower rungs of police force are also responsible for many of the excesses. As pointed out by Baxi, the police remain an "exploited, neglected and despised minority" who are denied the most basic minimum working conditions and who are "subservient to the rules rather than responsive to the people". The police are poorly paid, inadequately trained and face unrealistic pressure to produce high conviction rate. These conditions breed a tremendous degree of frustration discontentment and helplessness in the police force, which in some cases have resulted in police revolt e.g. PAC revolt in U.P. and police revolt in Haryana. Describing the pathetic and adverse condition in which the police have to work. A leader of an unofficial Police Association said:

> "We are the lowest paid among the Government employees, misused by politicians and officials alike, run around for twenty four hours and earn finally not two square meals bat a bad name from the public".

Most of the police personnel are political appointees whose main job is to make money and give part of it to their political patrons to keep them happy. Growing political interference often turns the police, the agents of ruling party- A former Director of the National Police Academy expressed his concern over this unfortunate situation in these words:

> "It now seems to be taken for granted that.... the police, would be available to the rating party to protect its supporters, to harass its opponents, and to further its

political interests... In many places the politicians, the police and lumpen elements have developed a vested interest. For the policeman who joins this combine it is both a means of enrichment and an insurance against punishment if exposed".

In cases in which the political bosses are interested the police are required to achieve instant result at all costs. This has contributed to and some times directly resulted in the police torturing suspect and political opponent even to death. What is most disturbing is the erroneous belief of majority of ministers, administrators and police officials about the inevitability and indispensability or third degree method. They seem to be convinced that third degree methods are the only effective means to deal with had characters and produce better results.

Lack of adequate and proper training and orientation pertaining to human rights, non-use and non-availability of scientific aids in investigation and interrogation, absence of effective system of intelligence collection, lack of necessary infrastructure in police stations, undersffating of the police stations and decay in criminal justice system have also contributed to the persistence of torture by the police during investigations and interrogations.

Remedial Measures

Following remedial measures need to be taken to halt the practice of torture by the police and create all effective institutional framework for the prevention of torture and other human rights violations."

(1) The Government should strengthen its international commitment to prevent torture which it affirmed when it ratified the Human Rights Covenants and agreed to the U.N. Declaration against Torture in

1979. In doing so, India declared it would comply with the U.N. Declaration against Torture and implement its provisions through legal and, other effective measures. The Government should now, like an increasing number of other countries through out the world accede to the U.N. convention against Torture and Other Cruel, Inhuman or Degrading Treatment or Punishment.

It will be a step in the right direction and affirmation of the country's determination to do away with torture. It will also send correct signals to the public servants, particularly members of the police and security forces not to transgress laws and rules of international conventions. The reasons put forward by the Central and State Governments for not acceding to the Convention are not convincing and any further delay in India's accession to the Convention will only provide a convenient handle to India's critics in international fora to severely indict it.

India should ratify or accede to the (first) Optional Protocol to the ICCPR, which allows individuals to complain to the Human Rights Committee for effective remedies after they have exhausted all domestic avenues for redress. The Government should remove the reservations it made when acceding to the ICCPR withholding from Indian citizens the right to compensation in case of wrongful arrest or detention. This is all the more necessary because the Supreme Court has already recognized the right to get compensation in such cases.

(2) The Government should launch an intensive programme of human rights education as a standard part of the training curriculum for all police and

security forces personnel involved in the arrest, detention and interrogation of suspects. Actual practices amounting to torture should be clearly spelled out under the Indian Police Act and other legal Instruments relating to treatment and training courses meant for the police personnel and members of the security forces should be restructured with the focus on human rights of the accused prisoners. The obligations undertaken by India with regard to promotion and protection of human rights and the abolition of torture and cruel, degrading inhuman treatment should be focused in the training programmes for the police personnel. Clear message should be given to police and the security forces that the use of torture shall not be tolerated under any circumstances, even in situations of emergency. Clear instructions should be given to all law enforcement personnel that orders from a superior officers are no defence against charges of torture. A system of incentives should be introduced for those who show care to protect the rights of, detainees and prisoners in their custody while the errant police personnel and the members of the security force should be sternly dealt with.

(3) Recommendations for police reforms such as those proposed by the Second Report of the National Police Commission 1979 and other expert bodies should he implemented to free the force from Political Influence and patronage and also constitute a statutory body such as State Security Commission in each State to help the State, Government "to discharge its superintending responsibility in an open manner, under the frameworks of law."

(4) At the time of arrest, the accused should necessarily be examined medically at the instance of the police. Failure of the accused to make the request for such medical examination under Section 54 of the Code of Criminal Procedure, should not exonerate the police from such liability.

(5) Judicial inquiries should be made mandatory into all allegations of torture, including rape and deaths in custody. The Government should ensure that prima-facie reports of torture, rape and deaths in custody published by the news media and by civil liberties groups are promptly and effectively investigated by an independent and impartial body. The Supreme Court and the High Courts should conduct their own inquiries whenever a victim alleges torture *or* illegal detention in a *habeas corpus* petition."

(6) The Government should order an authoritative investigation into the causes and the pattern of torture in India and the circumstances facilitating its widespread occurrence.

(7) There should be a statutory right to compensation. An effective machinery for redress for victims of torture and custodial deaths should be established. In its continuing effort to end custodial violence, it has taken the view that the compensation due to the *next* of kin of those who have died in custody should be the liability not just of the State Government, but of the offending police officials themselves. This should provide a further, powerful deterrent to aberrant behaviour by elements of the law enforcement machinery." Legal aid for the victims of abuses or their families should be easily available enabling them to live for compensation.

(8) The legal machinery to combat torture should be strengthened. The prohibition of torture and other cruel, inhuman or degrading treatment or punishment should be incorporated in the Constitution. The Government should formulate detailed guidelines for the interrogation of suspects and publish them after consulting with lawyers, bar association, civil liberties groups and medical professional groups. It should review these guidelines periodically in consultation with these groups to ensure that they are and remain an effective mechanism to prevent torture.

(9) The Government should make a public commitment that torture or ill treatment of detainees in custody or the police of security forces will not be tolerated and that it will ensure that such abuses will invariably lead to the perpetrators being brought to justice.

(10) Keeping in view the de-humanising aspect of the crime, the flagrant violation of the fundamental rights of the victim of the crime and the growing rise in the crimes of this type, where only a few come to light and others don't the Government and the legislature would have serious thought to the recommendation of the Law Commission and bring about appropriate changes in the system not only to curb the custodial crime but also to see that the custodial crime does not go unpunished."

(11) The courts are also required to have a change in their outlook and attitude, particularly in cases involving custodial crimes and they should exhibit more sensitivity and adopt a realistic approach rather than a narrow technical approach, while dealing with the cases of custodial crime *so* that as far as

possible within their powers, the guilty should not escape so that the victim of the crime has the satisfaction that ultimately the law has prevailed."

(12) Witnesses should be protected from intimidation and harassment and those accused of torture suspended from duty during such inquiries.

(13) Legal provisions in Section 6 or the Armed Forces (Special Powers) Act, 1958 granting the security forces immunity from prosecution and provisions inhibiting prosecutions of police officers-such as exist under Section 197 of the Code of Criminal Procedure-should be deleted.

(14) The duty to disobey superior orders to inflict torture-as provided in Article 5 of the U.N. Code of conduct for Law Enforcement Officials-should corporated in the Indian Police, Act.

(15) The right of detainees to have access to a medical examination, to request a judge or other independent body to order a second medical examination, and for victims of torture and their legal representatives to have access to the results of any medical examination should be incorporated in law.

(16) When examining reports on custodial death it was struck by the often unsatisfactory manner in which post-mortem examinations were conducted and reached the dismaying conclusion that, on occasion, the doctors concerned were bowing to police pressures when writing their reports. There was often a substantial time gap between the post-mortem examination and the writing of the reports; facilities in many mortuaries were abysmal; there was a lack of trained and qualified personnel. A system of further examine of post-mortem report would greatly minimise

to this kind of negligence. Recommendations for all post-mortem examinations in respect of deaths in police or jail custody to be video-filmed and the cassettes sent to the commission such as those proposed by the National Human Rights Commission should be implemented." Families of those who die in police custody should have the right to insist that a medical or other qualified person nominated by the family is present at the postmortem.

(17) The officers-in -charge of police stations should be instructed that all detainees must be formally notified of their rights. A list of the rights of all detainees in the local language should be displayed in all police-cells and other prominent places in police stations.

(18) For meeting the requirements of such genuine cases the Magistrate should be empowered to permit the investigating officer to further examine the accused in jail custody instead of the present practice of remanding him to police custody which puts him at times to risk of being tortured at the hands of a unscrupulous officer. This opportunity to further examine the accused in jail custody while protecting the interest of investigation would greatly minimise the scope for practising third degree.

(19) In order to establish liability of the police in cases of Custodial death the presumption of guilt should be raised against them."

(20) To look into and verify the complaints of custodial deaths, a Police Complaints Board consisting of a retired District and Sessions Judge (chairman) and a retired police officer of the rank of Superintendent of Police and a prominent citizen with administrative background as members should visit the scene and

ascertain the facts. If in its opinion, *a prime facia case* exists, a direction should be issued to the local chief of police to register a criminal case against the police personnel concerned and handover the case to the Crime Branch, CID, for further investigation. Whenever a death occurs in police custody, a judicial enquiry by the District and Session Judge should become mandatory."'

(21) A Judicial Magistrate should be available round the clock at a designated place in the city or town to attend to the judicial needs of the arrestees. He should be vested with all powers to grant bail, record confessions, issue judicial process etc. His presence and availability will automatically reduce the need for the police to hold the arrestees overnight or when the courts are closed:"

(22) There have been several such instances, in India of the *media* ably piloting the process of protecting human rights be tenaciously uncovering abuses. These have ranged from state violence, in the form of custodial deaths or fake encounters. The media provided publicity which led to successful public interest litigation, state intervention or community-action. The media must also promote popular recognition of all the rights enunciated by the Declaration, through regular discussion and debate. It is clear that role *of media* in safeguarding human rights is cardinal.

In addition to the above suggestions the following guidelines laid down by the Supreme Court in D.K. Basu v. Stale of W.B., are to he followed in all cases of arrest or detention till legislative measures are taken.

(i) The police personnel carrying out the arrest and

handling the interrogation of the arrestee should bear accurate, visible and clear identification and name tags with their designation. The particulars of all such police personnel who handle interrogation of the arrestee must be recorded in a register.

(ii) That the police officer carrying out the arrest of the arrestee shall prepare a memo of arrest at the time of arrest and such memo shall be attested by at least one witness, who may either be a member of the *family of the arrestee or a respectable* person of the locality from where the arrest is made. It shall also be countersigned by the arrestee and shall contain the time and date of arrest.

(iii) A person who has been arrested or detained and is being held in custody in a police station or interrogation centre or other lock-up, shall be entitled to have one friend or relative or other person known to him or having interest in his welfare being informed, as soon as practicable, that he has been arrested and is being detained at the particular place, unless the attesting witness of the memo of arrest is himself such a friend or a relative of the arrestee.

(iv) The time, place of arrest and venue of custody of an arrestee must be notified by the police where the next friend of relative of the arrestee lives outside the district or own through the Legal Aid Organization in the District and the police station of the area concerned telegraphically within a period of 9 to 12 hours after the arrest.

(v) The person arrested must be made aware of this right to have someone informed of his arrest or detention as soon as he is, put under arrest or is detained.

(vi) An entry must be made in the diary at the place of detention regarding the arrest of the person which shall also disclose the name of the next friend of the person who has been informed of the arrest and the names and particulars of the police officials in whose custody the arrestee is.

(vii) The arrestee should, where he so requests, be also examined at the time of his arrest and major and minor injuries, if any present of his her body, must be recorded at that time. The 'Inspection Memo" must be signed both by the arrestee and the police officer effecting the arrest and its copy provided to the arrestee.

(viii) The arrestee should be subjected to medical examination by a trained doctor every 48 hours during his detention in custody by a doctor on the panel of approved doctors appointed by Director, Health Services of the State or Union Territory concerned. Director, Health Services should prepare such a panel for all tehsils and districts as well.

(ix) Copies of all the documents including the memo of arrest, referred to above, should be sent to the area Magistrate for his record.

(x) The arrestee may be permitted to meet his lawyer during interrogation, though not throughout the interrogation,

(xi) A police control room should be provided at all district and State headquarters, where information regarding the arrest and the place of custody of the arrestee shall be communicated by the officer causing the arrest, within 12 hours of effecting the arrest and at the police control room it should be displayed on it conspicuous notice board

The court made it clear that failure to comply with the guidelines should, apart form rendering the official concerned liable for departmental action, also render him liable to contempt of the court.

In summary of the above remedial measures and guidelines it is clear that transparency of action and accountability perhaps are the possible safeguards which must insist upon. Attention is also required to be paid to properly develop work culture, training and orientation of the police force consistent with basic human values. Training methodology of the police needs restructuring. The force needs to be infused with basic human values and made sensitive to the constitutional ethos. Efforts must be made to change the attitude and approach of the police personnel handling investigations so they do not sacrifice basic human values during interrogation and do not resort to questionable forms of interrogation.

If these suggestions are acted upon in the right earnest, it would not only provide all effective control on the growing menace of custodial deaths and torture but would also develop the confidence of the people in the democratic system of the country besides improving the image of India in respect of human rights at the international level.

9

Disappearances

> "Circumstances are the rulers of the weak; they are but the instruments of the wise."
>
> —*Samuel Lover*

Some men arrive. They force their way into a family's home rich or poor, house, hovel or hut, in a city or in a village, anywhere. They come at any time of the day or night, usually in plain clothes, sometimes in uniform, always carrying weapons. Giving no reasons, producing no arrest warrant, frequently without saying who they are or on whose authority they are acting, they drag off one or more members of the family towards a car, using violence in the process if necessary.

This is often the first act in the drama of an enforced or involuntary disappearance, a particularly heinous violation of human rights. According to the Declaration on the Protection of All Persons from Enforced Disappearance, proclaimed by the General Assembly *in its* resolution 47/ 133 of 18 December 1992, an enforced disappearance occurs when "persons are arrested, detained or abducted against their will or otherwise deprived of their liberty by officials of different branches or levels of Government, or by organized groups, or private individuals acting on behalf of, or with the support, direct or indirect, consent or acquiescence of the Government, followed by a refusal to disclose the fate or whereabouts of the persons concerned or a refusal to acknowledge the deprivation of their liberty, which places such persons outside the protection of the law,'

A disappearance is a doubly paralysing form of suffering: for the victims, frequently tortured and in constant fear for their fives, and for their family members, ignorant of the fate of their loved ones, their emotions alternating between hope and despair, wondering and waiting, sometimes for years, for news that may never came. The victims are well aware that their families don't know what has become of them and that the chances are slim that anyone will come to their aid. Having been removed from the protective precinct of the law and "disappeared" from society, they are in fact deprived of all their rights and are at the mercy of their captors. If death is not the final outcome and they are eventually released from the nightmare, the victims may suffer a long time from the physical and psychological consequences of this from of dehumanization and from the brutality and torture which often accompany it.

The family and friends of disappeared persons experience slow mental tartars, not knowing whether the victim is still alive and, if so, where he or she is being held under what conditions, and in what state of health. Aware, furthermore, that they too are threatened-, that they may suffer the same fate themselves, and that to search for the truth may expose them to even greater danger.

The family's distress is frequently compounded by the material consequences resulting from the disappearance. The missing person is often the mainstay of the family's finances. He or she may be the only member of the family able to cultivate the crops or run the family business. The emotional upheaval is thus exacerbated by material deprivation, made more acute by the costs incurred should they decide to undertake a search. Furthermore, they do not know when - if ever - their loved one is going to return, which makes it difficult for them to adapt to the new situation. In some cases, national legislation may make it impossible to receive pensions or other means of support in the absence of a certificate of death. Economic and social marginalization are frequently the result.

Rights Violated by the Practice of Disappearance

The practice of enforced disappearance of persons infringes upon an entire range of human rights embodied in the Universal Declaration of Human Rights and set out in both International Covenants on Human Rights as well as in other major international human rights instruments.

Disappearances can also involve serious violations of the Standard Minimum Rules for the Treatment of Prisoners, approved by the United Nations Economic and Social Council in 1957, as well as in the Code of Conduct for Law Enforcement Officials and the Body of Principals for the Protection of All Persons under Any Form of Detention or Imprisonment, adopted, by the General Assembly in 1979 and 1988 respectively. The following individual rights may also be infringed upon in the course of a disappearance:

- The right to recognition as a person before the law;
- The right to liberty and the security of the person;
- The right not to be subjected to torture and other cruel, inhuman or degrading treatment or punishment;
- The right to life.

Disappearances generally violate the right to a family life as well as various economic, social and cultural rights such as the right to an adequate standard of living and the right to education. In fact, it has been found that the disappearance of the family's main economic support, particularly in less affluent societies, frequently leaves the family in a desperate socio-economic situation in which the majority of the rights enumerated in the International Covenant on Economic, Social and Cultural Rights cannot be realized.

The serious economic hardships which usually accompany a disappearance are most often borne by women. When women are the victims of disappearance they become particularly vulnerable to sexual and other forms of violence. In addition, it is women who are most often at the forefront of the struggle to resolve the disappearances of members of their family. In this capacity they may suffer intimidation, persecution and reprisals.

Children are also involved in disappearances, both directly and indirectly. The disappearance of a child is a clear contravention of a number of provisions of the Convention on the Rights of the Child, including the right to a personal identity. The loss of a parent through disappearance is also a serious violation of a child's human rights.

Working Group on and Forced or Involuntary Disappearances

Given the grave nature of disappearances, the United Nations General Assembly devoted particular attention to this odious phenomenon. In 1979, in resolution 33/173 entitled "Disappeared persons", in which it expressed concern over reports from various parts of the world relating to enforced or involuntary disappearances of persons, the Assembly requested the United Nations Commission on Human Rights to consider the question and to make appropriate recommendations.

At that time the Assembly also called upon Governments to devote appropriate resources to undertake rapid and impartial investigations into cases of enforced or involuntary disappearances and to ensure that law enforcement and security authorities were fully accountable, especially in law, in the discharge of their duties. Such accountability would include legal responsibility for unjustifiable excesses which might lead to enforced or involuntary disappearances and to other violations of human rights.

By resolution 20 (XXXVI) of 29 February 1980, the Commission an Human V Rights decided to "establish for a period of one year a working group consisting of five of its members, to serve as experts in their individual capacities, to examine questions relevant to enforced or involuntary disappearances of persons". Since then, the mandate and terms of reference of the Working Group have been renewed by the Commission and approved by the Economic and Social Council each year. Since 1986 this has been done biennially and, since 1992, on a three-yearly basis.

The establishment in 1980 of the Working Group on Enforced or Involuntary Disappearances by the Commission on Human Rights, inspired by the General Assembly, was the first thematic mechanism set up within the framework of the United Nations Human Rights Programme to deal with specific violations of human rights of a particularly serious nature occurring on a global scale. Previous to that, working groups and special rapporteurs had been appointed only to deal with the human rights situation in a given country or territory,

Subsequent years have seen the establishment, by the Commission or the Secretary- General, of other so-called thematic procedures in related fields, such as the appointment of special rapporteurs/representatives on extrajudicial, summary or arbitrary executions; the question of torture; the independence of judges and lawyers; internally displaced persons; freedom of opinion and expression; violence against women; intolerance and discrimination based on religion or belief; racism, racial discrimination and xenophobia-, the effects of toxic and dangerous products on the enjoyment of human rights; the sale of children, child prostitution and child pornography; the use of mercenaries; and the establishment of the Working Group on Arbitrary Detention.

Since its inception, the Working Group on Enforced or Involuntary Disappearances has dealt with some 50,000 individual cases pertaining to more than 70 countries. For reasons well beyond the scope of the Working Group, only a fraction of those cases have been clarified. Nevertheless, the extent to which the Working Group, through its patient and persistent contacts with the Governments concerned, may have prevented more cases from occurring cannot be quantified. The fact that it was able to contribute to the clarification of cases, especially within the framework of its urgent action procedure (see below), and thus possibly to the saving of human lives, has been considered sufficient reason for its continued activity.

Moreover, the mechanism of the Working Group should be seen as a reflection of international concern and action. It should equally be seen as forming part of a long-term process leading to the elimination of major human rights violations, a process which includes the creation of widespread public awareness of human rights-related issues and the provision of advisory services and technical assistance to

Governments for the promotion and protection of human rights.

In its annual resolutions on the subject the Commission on Human Rights has endorsed the Working Group's methods of work and the humanitarian spirit underlying its mandate. It has urged the Governments concerned to take steps to protect the families of disappeared persons against any intimidation or ill-treatment to which they might be subjected and encouraged them to give serious consideration to inviting the Working Group to visit their country. It also stressed the importance of publicizing the objectives, procedures and methods of the Working Group within the framework of the information activities of the United Nations Centre for Human Rights.

The Commission has also requested the Working Group to take action in connection with acts of intimidation or reprisals against relatives of missing persons and private individuals or groups who seek to cooperate or have cooperated with United Nations human rights bodies, or who have provided testimony or information to them, as well as persons who avail or have availed themselves of procedures established under United Nations auspices for the protection of human rights and fundamental freedoms or persons who have provided legal assistance to others for that purpose.

Activities of the Working Group

The Working Group's basic mandate is to assist the relatives of disappeared persons to ascertain the fate and whereabouts of their missing family members. For this purpose the Group receives and examines reports of disappearances submitted by relatives of missing persons or human rights organizations acting on their behalf. After determining whether those reports comply with a number of criteria, the

Working Group transmits individual cases to the Governments concerned, requesting them to carry out investigations and to inform the Working Group of the results. The Working Group deals with the numerous individual cases of human rights violations on a purely humanitarian basis, irrespective of whether the Government concerned has ratified any of the existing legal instruments which provide for an individual complaints procedure. It acts essentially as a channel of communication between the families of missing persons and Governments, and has successfully developed a dialogue with the majority of Governments concerned with the aim of solving cases of disappearance.

With a view to preventing irreparable damage, the Working Group has also established an urgent action procedure under which the Working Group's Chairman is authorized to act on reported cases of disappearance occurring in between the Group's sessions, thus helping to avoid any delays in its attempts to save lives.

Cases of intimidation, persecution or reprisals against relatives of missing persons, witnesses to disappearances or their families, members of organizations of relatives and other non-governmental organizations or individuals concerned with disappearances are also transmitted to the pertinent Governments, with an appeal to take the necessary steps to protect all the fundamental rights of the persons concerned.

The Working Group meets three times a year for five to eight working days, once in New York and twice in Geneva. The Group's meetings are held in private. However, the Working Group regularly invites representatives of Governments, non-governmental organizations, family members and witnesses to meet with it. Following each session, the Working Group informs Governments, in writing, of decisions taken with regard to disappearances in their country. It reminds Governments, at least once a year, of the total number of cases transmitted in the past which have not yet been clarified. Twice a year it reminds Governments of urgent action cases sent during the preceding six months for which no clarification has been received.

The Working Group reports annually to the Commission on Human Rights on the activities it has carried put since the Commission's previous session, up until the last day of the Working Group's third annual session. It informs the Commission of its communications with Governments and non-governmental organizations, its meetings and its missions. The Working Group reports on all cases of disappearance received by the Group during the year, on a country-by-country basis, and on the decisions it has taken thereon. It provides the Commission with a statistical summary for each country of cases transmitted to the Government, clarifications made and the status of the person concerned on the date of clarification. It includes graphs showing the development of the phenomenon of disappearance in countries with more than 50 transmitted cases, up to the date of the adoption by the Working Group of its annual report. The Working Group includes conclusions and recommendations in its report, and makes observations on the situation of disappearances in individual countries. Since 1993, the Group also has reported on the implementation of the Declaration on the Protection of All Persons from Enforced Disappearance and the obstacles encountered therein, and periodically reports on broader issues surrounding the phenomenon of disappearance.

Methods of Work of the Working Group

The methods of work of the Working Group are based

on its mandate as stipulated in Commission on Human Rights resolution 20 (XXXVI) and are specifically geared to its main objective: to assist families in determining the fate and whereabouts of their missing relatives who, having disappeared, are outside the protection of the law. To this end, the Working Group endeavours to establish a channel of communication between the families and the Governments concerned, seeking to ensure that sufficiently documented and clearly identified individual cases which the families, directly or indirectly, have brought to the Working Group's attention are investigated and the whereabouts of the missing person clarified.

The Working Group's role ends when the fate and whereabouts of the missing person have been clearly established as a result of investigations by the Government or the family, irrespective of whether that person is alive or dead. At that point the Working Group no longer concerns itself with the question of determining responsibility for specific cases of disappearance or for other human rights violations which may have occurred in the course of a disappearance; its work on this individual level is of a strictly humanitarian nature.

The Working Group's action is based on the principle that the State is responsible for human rights violations committed within its territory and is obligated to prevent such violations or to investigate them when they have occurred. As with all other situations of State responsibility, such responsibility continues to exist irrespective of changes of Government.

The Working Group does not deal with situations of international armed conflict, in view of the competence of the International Committee of the Red Cross (ICRC) in such situations, as determined by the Geneva Conventions of 12 August 1949 and their Additional Protocols of 1977. Further information on these conventions may be found in Fact Sheet *No.* 13: International Humanitarian Law and Human Rights.

In considering cases of disappearance, the Working Group deals exclusively with Governments because, as explained above, Governments must, as a matter of principle, assume responsibility for violations of human rights occurring on their territory. The Working Group will not consider cases of abductions which are not directly or indirectly attributable to a Government. It will therefore not process individual cases of disappearances perpetrated by irregular or insurgent groups fighting a Government on its own territory. Nevertheless, when studying the situation of disappearances in a particular country or examining the phenomenon of disappearance in a general way, the Working Group considers that information on all disappearances is relevant to a proper evaluation.

Admissibility

For a report of a disappearance to be considered admissible by the Working Group, it must originate from the family or friends of the missing person. Such reports may also be channelled to the Working Group through representatives of the family, Governments, intergovernmental organizations, humanitarian organizations and other reliable sources. They must be submitted in writing with a clear indication of the identity of the sender. If the source is other than a family member, it must be in a position to follow up with the relatives of the disappeared person concerning his or her fate.

In order to enable the Governments named in the reports

to carry out meaningful investigations, the Working Group provides them with information containing at least a minimum of basic data. In addition, the Working Group constantly urges the sources of reports to furnish as many details as possible on the identity of the missing person (even, if available, the identity card number) and the circumstances of the disappearance. The following minimum elements are required:

(a) Full name of the missing person;

(b) Date of disappearance, i.e. day, month and year of arrest or abduction or day, month and year when the missing person was last seen. If the missing person was last seen in a detention centre, an approximate indication is sufficient, (c) Place of arrest or abduction or where the missing person was last seen (at least an indication of the town or village);

(d) Parties presumed to have carried out the arrest or abduction or to hold the missing person in unacknowledged detention; and,

(e) Steps taken to determine the fate or whereabouts of the missing person, or at least an indication that efforts to use domestic remedies were frustrated or otherwise inconclusive.

Handling of Cases

Reported cases of disappearance are placed before the Working Group for detailed examination during its sessions. Those which fulfil the requirements as outlined above are transmitted, with the Working Group's specific authorization, to the Governments concerned, with a request to carry out investigations and to inform the Working Group of the results.

The cases are normally communicated by letter from the Working Group's Chairman to the Government concerned through that Government's Permanent Representative to the United Nations. However, cases that occurred within three months preceding the receipt of the report of the disappearance by the Working Group are transmitted directly to the Minister for Foreign Affairs of the country concerned by the most direct and rapid means. This is referred to as the urgent action procedure. Such communications can be authorized by the Chairman on the basis of specific authority delegated to him by the Working Group. Cases which occurred prior to the three-months limit but not more than one year before the date of their receipt by the secretariat can be transmitted between sessions by letter, upon authorization by the Chairman, provided that they have some connection with a case which occurred within the three-month period.

Reports indicating that officials from more than one country were directly responsible for or involved in a disappearance are communicated to both the Government of the country where the disappearance occurred and the Government of the country whose officials or agents were alleged to have participated in the arrest or abduction of the missing person. However, in any general evaluation of disappearances in a given country which may be made, such cases are attributed to the country in which the person was reportedly held in detention or last seen.

In cases of the disappearance of a pregnant woman, the child presumed to have been born during the mother's captivity is mentioned in the description of the mother's case. The child is treated as a separate case when witnesses have reported that the mother actually gave birth during her detention.

The Working Group reminds every Government concerned at least once a year of the cases which have not yet been clarified, and twice a year of all urgent action cases transmitted during the preceding six months for which no clarification has been received. Furthermore, at any time during the year any Government may request, in writing, the summaries of cases that the Group has transmitted to it.

Replies from Governments and Clarification of Cases

Any reply from the Government containing detailed information on the fate and whereabouts of a disappeared person is transmitted to the source. If the source does not respond within six months of the date on which the Government's reply was communicated to it, or if it contests the Government's information on grounds which are considered unreasonable by the Working Group, the case is considered clarified and is accordingly listed under the heading "Cases clarified by the Government's response" in the statistical summary of the annual report. If the source contests the Government's information on reasonable grounds, the Government is so informed and asked to comment.

If the source provides well-documented information that a case has erroneously been considered clarified because the Government's reply referred to a different person, does not correspond to the reported situation or has not reached the source within the six-month period described above, the Working Group resubmits the case to the Government, requesting it to comment. In such instances the case is again listed among the unclarified cases and a specific explanation of the situation is given in the Working Group's report to the Commission on Human Rights, indicating the errors or discrepancies. Any additional substantive information which the source submits on an outstanding case is placed before the Working Group and, following its approval, transmitted to the Government concerned. If the additional information received amounts to a clarification of the case, the Government is so informed.

The Working Group retains cases in its files as long as the exact whereabouts of the missing persons have not been determined. It maintain- that the State's responsibility for disappearances continues to exist irrespective of changes of Government, even though the new Government shows greater respect for human rights than the Government in power at thy time the violations occurred. The Working Group will agree to close a case in its files when the competent authority specified in the relevant national law pronounces, with the concurrence of the relatives and other interested parties, that the person reported missing is presumed dead. In exceptional circumstances the Working Group may decide to discontinue consideration of a case which the families have decided not to pursue, or where the source is no longer in existence or unable to follow up the case.

While the Working Group's mandate does not extend beyond the stage at which a disappeared person's fate is made known, other human rights procedures of the United Nations can take up where the Working Group leaves off. If the reply from the Government concerned clearly indicates that the missing person has been found dead, tortured, in arbitrary but acknowledged detention, or to be a victim of other human rights violations for which government officials or groups or individuals linked to them are allegedly responsible, the case is brought to the attention of the appropriate mechanism or body.

Protection of Relatives and Witnesses

The Working Group is also concerned with the protection

of relatives of missing persons, their legal counsel, witnesses to disappearances or their family, members of organizations of relatives and other non-governmental organizations or individuals concerned with disappearances.

In cases of persecution, intimidation or reprisals against these persons, the Working Group contacts the Government concerned with the appeal that they take all necessary steps to protect the fundamental rights of the persons concerned and to investigate the case thoroughly in order to put an end to the intimidation or reprisals.

Prompt intervention is often required to protect relatives, witnesses and other persons involved in a disappearance. Allegations of intimidation, persecution or reprisals are transmitted directly to the relevant Ministers of Foreign Affairs by the most direct and rapid means. The Working Group has authorized its Chairman to transmit such information between sessions.

Declaration on the Protection of All Persons from Enforced Disappearance

On 18 December 1992 the General Assembly, by resolution 47/133, proclaimed the Declaration on the Protection of All Persons from Enforced Disappearance. The Working Group, which participated actively in the elaboration of the Declaration, welcomed it as a milestone in the united efforts to combat the practice of disappearance and considered that it constituted an important basis for its own future work. Many proposals and recommendations which the Working Group had adopted over the years and published in its annual reports were reflected in the Declaration.

According to the Declaration, the systematic practice of disappearance is of the nature of a crime against humanity and constitutes a violation of the right to recognition as a person before the law, the right to liberty and security of the person, and the right not to be subjected to torture; it also violates or constitutes a grave threat to the right to life. States are under an obligation to take effective legislative, administrative, judicial or other measures to prevent and terminate acts of enforced disappearance, in particular to make them continuing offences under criminal law and to establish civil liability.

The Declaration also refers to the right to a prompt and effective judicial remedy as well as unhampered access by national authorities to all places of detention, the right to habeas corpus, the maintenance of centralized registers of all persons in detention, the duty to investigate fully all alleged cases of disappearance, the duty to try alleged perpetrators of disappearances before ordinary (not military) courts, the exemption of the criminal offence of acts of enforced disappearance from ordinary statutes of limitations and special amnesty laws and simllar measures which might lead to impunity.

The World Conference on Human Rights, held at Vienna from 14 to 25 June 1993, welcomed the adoption of the Declaration by the General Assembly and called upon all States "to take effective legislative, administrative, judicial or other measures to prevent, terminate and punish acts of enforced disappearances". The World Conference reaffirmed that "it is the duty of all States, under any circumstances, to make investigations whenever there is reason to believe that an enforced disappearance has taken place on a territory under their jurisdiction and, if allegations are confirmed, to prosecute its perpetrators".

Since 1993, the Commission on Human Rights has regularly adopted resolutions in which it invited all

Governments to take appropriate legislative or other steps to prevent and punish the practice of enforced disappearances, with special reference to the Declaration, and to take action to that end nationally, regionally and in cooperation with the United Nations. In the same resolutions, the Commission requested the Working Group to take into account the provisions of the Declaration, and invited it to cite in future reports any obstacles to the proper application of the Declaration and to recommend means of overcoming them.

Despite various efforts by the Working Group to remind Governments of their obligation to implement the provisions of the Declaration by taking appropriate legislative, administrative, judicial or other measures, very little progress has been made in practice. With some exceptions. States have not begun to take consistent steps to incorporate the principles set out in the Declaration in their national legislation. The Working Group has repeatedly stressed that the obligation to implement the Declaration applies not only to States where acts of enforced disappearances actually occurred in the past or have continued up to the present day; in particular, legislative and other preventive measures shall be taken by all States in order to ensure that acts of disappearance will not occur in the future.

The Working Group regularly transmits to the Governments concerned a summary of allegations received from relatives of missing persons and non-governmental organizations with regard to violations of the Declaration in their respective country, inviting them to comment thereon if they so wish.

Affirmative Actions to Abolish Torture, Disappearances, and Extra-Legal Executions

In 1989, the world witnessed a cataclysm of events,

Dictatorships fell; walls were torn; countries invaded. While some countries experienced rapid transformations, other countries-mostly belonging to the Third World-found themselves more deeply entrenched in poverty, their citizen's basic human rights increasingly trampled with impunity.

Publicly claiming adherence to human rights and the rule of law while actually selling aside-and conveniently forgetting—the wealth of national and international instruments which they ratified, third world governments continue to be reigned with terror." And government by terror is the response of Third World States, which are clients of one or the other super power, to the stresses of economic development, economic crisis, or the East-West confrontation". The ideology of terror is a response to what governments view as world realpolitik, represented by the three fundamental precepts of geopolitics, total strategy and the privileged role or the armed forces. World realpolitik, as viewed by Third World States, is perhaps best explained by the following propositions:

1. The world is divided into two blocs, the East and the West, whose values and interests are irreconcilably opposed.
2. The conflict between them is not only military, but also a struggle against the ideology, culture and traditions of the adversary.
3. The conflict occurs not only internationally but also intranationally.
4. The duty of the military authorities to defend the nation therefore extends to the combat against, any quasi-military, ideological, cultural or other manifestations of this enemy within the country,

making whatever sacrifices in the rights of citizens or alterations in the structure of government this may require"

These propositions also broadly compose the doctrine of national security", used by most Third World States to justify their existence. Central to the ideology of terror or the doctrine of national security is the pre-emptive control of citizens and ideas in order to ensure the internal economic status quo which benefits those in power-and to guarantee some form of economic activity which benefits not only those in power, but also, and more importantly, those foreign governments which support, encourage and prop up the ruling regime.

Under the ideology of terror of the doctrine of national security, human persons are not important. "Rather they are utilized as tools and tally beads in international competition where aggregate figures count for more than personhood". Individual needs are subservient to "national security imperatives"; fuller human development and human values are restricted and subverted by the dominance of security priorities, such as military force, economic power and control of the population. "Equating the political or ideological opponent with an enemy not entitled to respect for the 'inherent dignity of the human person', but whose only entitlement is to a combat without quarter, is perhaps the most destructive legacy of the doctrine of national security".

State terrorism is deeply rooted in relatively permanent structures of society that allow terror to be institutionalized. So that, even if countries experience changes in the composition and even the nature of their governments, such as the Philippines, for example, state terrorism still flourishes because the structures that nurture it remain intact.

These structures include the imposition of emergency rule or martial law; emergency legislations broadening powers of the ruling regime; enlargement of the military to exceptional numbers, and increasing their powers, scope of activities and access to records; assigning civil functions to the military and police establishment; abrogation of constitutional rights and freedoms, particularly free press and assembly and the rights of workers; emasculation of the judiciary; denial of due process of law by resorting to warrantless arrests, unexplained disappearances and extra legal executions; fostering a siege of war mentality; allowing and encouraging the free flow of material aid and training by foreign governments supporting the regime to the regime in power, suspension *of habeas corpus* and other legal remedies; subverting legal processes by requiring trials of civilians in military courts; granting immunity to security officers; enacting laws which provide for preventive detention and which change the law of evidence; and the politicization of human rights.

Torture, enforced disappearances and summary executions are inherent to government by terror. They are part and parcel of government's security strategy. They are effective instruments and widely used political tools to control the population, to stifle all forms and manner of dissent, and to maintain and strengthen the internal political, economic and cultural status quo.

These practices are not limited to particular governments; governments cooperate with each other to exchange information "and act in concert to arrest and liquidate each others' dissidents who happen to come within their jurisdiction".

Governments that do not practice torture, enforced

disappearances or extra-judicial executions, but support and provide material aid and training to regimes that do, in effect, also engage in these abominable practices. They are accomplices to the acts perpetrated by Third World States against their citizens. In fact, "....[f]inancing police states-and all the horrors that implies-is a conscious and deliberate political and economic policy [of the United States Government] .... [And] [i]t has been proven over and over that it is impossible for a country to be dependent on an outside power and remain a healthy democracy on the inside".

Despite national and international prohibition, torture, involuntary disappearances and extra legal executions still occur. Since these repugnant practices are perpetrated by public officials and state agents, with or without official government sanction, it is quite clear that government, on its own, will not act to abolish these heinous practices. It is therefore incumbent on the people, and particularly on human rights workers, to undertake affirmative action to abolish torture, summary executions and the practice of involuntary disappearances. In order to abolish these unconscionable practices-and the structures which nurture and sustain them-we must devise a two-pronged simultaneous inter-locking campaign; one addressed to help victims-obtain redress and the other towards creating conditions that would effectively prohibit these practices.

The first part of our campaign— helping victims obtain redress—could be accomplished by mobilizing the medical and legal professions, and by campaigning for an effective complaints machinery. Doctors should be encouraged to medically document evidence of torture, and to conduct autopsies, and should be approached to testify before the courts. Lawyers should maximize existing legal remedies, such as filing criminal, civil or special relief proceedings against those who perpetrate these practices, and their immediate superiors.

Our efforts should also be directed towards the creation of a complaints machinery. The key elements of an effective complaints machinery are: its impartial and civilian composition; clear terms of reference; public, speedy and prompt disposition of complaints, vigorous, active and conscientious pursuit of offenders, simple and easily accessible procedures for filing complaints', protection of witnesses and complainants, and guarantee *of* the right to *file,* complaints.

The second part of our campaign is directed towards creating, on structural, administrative, procedural, national and international levels, such conditions necessary for the abolition of these practices. This is the more difficult, albeit more challenging aspect of our campaign.

On the structural level, we must campaign for a national law prohibiting these practices, for the repeat of various existing laws which encourage these practices, and the enactment of new laws and codes of conduct.

In order to effectively ban these practices, a national law prohibiting them-in addition to safeguards in national constitutions-is today essential. The law against torture, involuntary disappearances, and summary executions, which should clearly stipulate that these practices are crimes against humanity, must recognize three basic principles:

1. That government is legally responsible for repairing damages suffered by victims and their families, and for prosecuting and punishing all who, by complicity or negligence, are responsible for torturing, executing or forcing one to disappear who is in government

custody or under interrogation by government agents, regardless of the motives of the perpetrators;

2. That no pardon or amnesty may be granted to any person accused of these practices since these practices are universal and imprescriptible offences;
3. That governments who do not themselves engage in these practices, but supply governments that do with the tools or the know-how, are accessories before the fact and, as such, are responsible for the results.

We must also work actively and speedily for the immediate repeal of existing laws which encourage these practices. Such laws would include: all emergency legislation; those that provide for preventive or administrative detention; those that permit waivers of rights to counsel and to remain silent; and such laws of evidence that rely heavily on confessions and create additional incentives to obtain confessions.

We must also endeavour to enact new innovative national laws and codes of conduct which clearly ban torture, enforced disappearances and extra-judicial executions. We must strive towards the immediate enactment of Codes of Professional Ethical Conduct for law enforcement officials (military, police and civilian components), for the medical profession and for the legal profession which contain clear official directives condemning and banning these practices, and which prescribe strict ethical rules and guidelines on their relationship with and conduct towards all persons in government custody. We must campaign for the enactment of a Code for the Treatment of Detainees.

We must also campaign for the enactment of new laws which call not only for the suspension from office or all charged with perpetrating these acts but also for their disqualification from promotion, automatic or otherwise, during the pendency of the complaint; and for a law which disciplines immediate superiors of officers or soldiers/ policemen who are found guilty of these acts unless said immediate superiors show that they have taken every reasonable precaution to prevent them.

On the administrative level, we must also work towards the creation of practical measures reinforcing supervision and accountability of persons involved in detention and interrogation.

The practical measures would include:

- a central register of all arrests and detentions;
- prompt reporting of all arrests and detentions to the judicial authorities and to the families and lawyers of all persons arrested, and to any interested parties; such reports should include at least the date, time, place and cause of the arrest, the identity of the arresting officer, his official station and authority to effect the arrest, the place where the person arrested is detained, and the name of the officer in charge thereof;
- a ban on incommunicado detentions, secret detention pi aces and secret arrests;
- immediate notification, upon arrest, to the person arrested of his rights;
- immediate medical examination of person arrested, and periodic and regular medical examinations, by physicians of choice, of all persons arrested, detained and in custody;
- unimpaired and immediate access to civil courts;

- unrestricted regular visits by family, friends, lawyers, doctors and religious advisers, without delay or hinderance;
- systematic review of interrogation rules, instructions, methods, procedures and practices, as well as arrangements for custody and treatment of detainees;
- periodic inspections of detention centers, jails, prisons and all other places of detention, and interviews of persons under detention by impartial and independent national and international governmental or nongovernmental organizations;
- the release of persons arrested only to their families, and when they have no families, to a responsible civilian. Releases must be accompanied by a "certificate of Release", executed by the officer in charge of the detention center; copies of the "Certificate of Release" must be immediately furnished to the family of the person released, and to the judicial authorities;
- where there is evidence of arrest or other manner of apprehension of a person, by officers of the law, and such person is not thereafter seen nor heard from, the officer or officers who effected the apprehension should be held accountable to explain the disappearance without delay.

On the procedural level, we must work actively towards strengthening the judiciary in cases involving torture, unexplained disappearences and extralegal executions. "The ordinary courts should retain jurisdiction over changes of abuse of power by security forces, since entrusting jurisdiction over such offences to military or security courts has proven ineffective in preventing such abuse, and may even amount to a *de facto* grant of immunity which encourage human rights violations .... There is nothing more likely to ensure repetition... than the knowledge by the offenders that an official veil of secrecy will be drawn over their crimes" [International Commission of Jurists. States Emergency, 1983]. The judiciary should undertake speedy, public and impartial investigations of all such complaints, retain unimpaired the right to complain without limits in space and time, retain unimpaired and enforceable the right to seek a fair and adequate compensation and rehabilitation, provide adequate protection for complainants and witnesses, and require that all offenders be tried in civil courts.

On the national level, we should conduct public campaigns against these practices and vigorous education and training on the prohibition of these practices, directed to the general public, and to the police, military, para-military and other investigative personnel.

Our public campaigns should be creative, innovative and effective. These could include publicity of individual accounts, international exposure of all such cases, circulation of public appeals and/or petitions addressed to various government officials and agencies, fasting, vigils, public demonstrations, dissemination of posters, stickers, buttons and the like. Our public campaigns should be geared towards generating public abhorrence of these practices and support and sympathy for the various structural, administrative, procedural, national and international aspects of our general campaign.

We should also conduct training and education against these practices for the general public. Teachers should be encouraged to discuss them in their classes. Priests and pastors should be encouraged to discuss them in their pulpits, And we should campaign for the continuous education and training of police, para-military personnel, medical personnel, public officials, and other persons involved in the custody, interrogation or treatment of any person subjected to any form of arrest, detention or imprisonment.

And finally, on the international level, we must activity and vigorously purse affirmative action directed against these governments which support, encourage and provide the equipment, expertise, tools and technical or other know-how to other governments and armed forces, to violate their citizens. Our actions could be directed towards the population of that government, to create awareness among their citizens of the actions their governments take which adversely affect the citizens of these terror regimes, to spur their population to pressure their own governments to cease their complicity in these acts, and to encourage their population to seek a halt to all forms of military aid to our governments. We could also exert pressure on such governments to cease their dependency on that government, and to reject all forms of military aid.

There is much left to be done. Whether we shall be successful or not, only time, and our activities will tell. But if we do not act now, we, our children, and our children's children, will reap the burdens of our inactivity.

We have a responsibility to ourselves, to our children, and to the unborn generations to come, to create a humane and decent, society. We cannot— we should not—fail.

APPENDICES

APPENDIX–I

CONVENTION AGAINST TORTURE AND OTHER CRUEL, INHUMAN OR DEGRADING TREATMENT OR PUNISHMENT

The States Parties to this Convention,

Considering that, in accordance with the principles proclaimed in the Charter of the United Nations, recognition of the equal and inalienable rights of all members of the human family is the foundation of freedom, justice and peace in the world,

Recognizing that those rights derive from the inherent dignity of the human person,

Considering the obligation of States under the Charter, in particular Article 55, to promote universal respect for and observance of, human rights and fundamental freedoms,

Having regard to article 5 of the Universal Declaration of Human Rights and article 7 of the International Covenant on Civil and Political Rights, both of which provide that no one shall be subjected to torture or to cruel, inhuman or degrading treatment or punishment,

Having regard also to the Declaration on the Protection of All Persons from Being Subjected to Torture and Other Cruel, Inhuman or Degrading Treatment or Punishment, adopted by the General Assembly on 9 December 1975,

Desiring to make more effective the struggle against torture and other cruel, inhuman or degrading treatment or punishment throughout the world,

Have agreed as follows..

PART I

Article 1

1. For the purposes of this Convention, the term "torture" means any act by which severe pain or suffering, whether physical or mental, is intentionally inflicted on a person for such purposes as obtaining from him or a third person information or a confession, punishing him for an act he or a third person has committed or is suspected of having committed, or intimidating or coercing him or a third person, or for any reason based on discrimination of any kind, when such pain or suffering is inflicted by or at the instigation of or with the consent or acquiescence of a public official or other person acting in an official capacity. It does not include pain or suffering arising only from, inherent in or incidental to lawful sanctions.
2. This article is without prejudice to any international instrument or national legislation which does or may contain provisions of wider application.

Article 2

1. Each State Party shall take effective legislative, administrative, judicial or other measures to prevent acts of torture in any territory under its jurisdiction.
2. No exceptional circumstances whatsoever, whether a state of war or a threat of war, internal political instability or any other public emergency, may be invoked as a justification of torture.

3. An order from a superior officer or a public authority may not be invoked as a justification of torture.

Article 3

1. No State Party shall expel, return ("refouler") or extradite a person to another State where there are substantial grounds for believing that he would be in danger of being subjected to torture.
2. For the purpose of determining whether there are such grounds, the competent authorities shall take into account all relevant considerations including, where applicable, the existence in the State concerned of a consistent pattern of gross, flagrant or mass violations of human rights.

Article 4

1. Each State Party shall ensure that all acts of torture are offences under its criminal law. The same shall apply to an attempt to commit torture and to an act by any person which constitutes complicity or participation in torture.
2. Each State Party shall make these offences punishable ay appropriate penalties which take into account their grave nature,

Article 5

1. Each State Party shall take such measures as may be necessary to establish its jurisdiction over the offences referred to in article 4 in the following cases:
   (a) When the offences are committed in any territory under its jurisdiction or on board a ship or aircraft registered in that State;
   (b) When the alleged offender is a national of that State;

(c) When the victim is a national of that State if that State considers it appropriate.

2. Each State Party shall likewise take such measures as may be necessary to establish its jurisdiction over such offences in cases where the alleged offender is present in any territory under its jurisdiction and it does not extradite him pursuant to article 8 to any of the States mentioned in paragraph *I* of this article,

3. This Convention does not exclude any criminal jurisdiction exercised in accordance with internal law.

Article 6

1. Upon being satisfied, after an examination of information available to it, that the circumstances so warrant, any State Party in whose territory a person alleged to have committed any offence referred to in article 4 is present shall take him into custody or take other legal measures to ensure his presence. The custody and other legal measures shall be as provided in the law of that State but may be continued only for such time as is necessary to enable any criminal or extradition proceedings to be instituted:

2. Such State shall immediately make a preliminary inquiry into the facts.

3. Any person in custody pursuant to paragraph 1 of this article shall be assisted in communicating immediately with the nearest appropriate representative of the State of which he is a national, or, if he is a stateless person, with the representative of the State where he usually resides.

4. When a State, pursuant to this article, has taken a person into custody, it shall immediately notify the

States referred to in article 5, paragraph 1, of the fact that such person is in custody and of the circumstances which warrant his detention. The State which makes the preliminary inquiry contemplated in paragraph 2 of this article shall promptly report its findings to the said States and shall indicate whether it intends to exercise jurisdiction.

Article 7

1. The State Party in the territory under whose jurisdiction a person alleged to have committed any offence referred to in article 4 is found shall in the cases contemplated in article 5, if it does not extradite him, submit the case to its competent authorities for the purpose of prosecution.
2. These authorities shall take their decision in the same manner as in the case of any ordinary offence of a serious nature under the law of that State. In the cases referred to in article 5, paragraph 2, the standards of evidence required for prosecution and conviction shall in no way be less stringent than those which apply in the cases referred to in article 5, paragraph 1.
3. Any person regarding whom proceedings are brought in connection with any of the offences referred to in article 4 shall be guaranteed fair treatment at all stages of the proceedings.

Article 8

1. The offences referred to in article 4 shall be deemed to be included as extraditable offences in any extradition treaty existing between States Parties. States Parties undertake to include such offences as extraditable

offences in every extradition treaty to be concluded between them.

2. If a State Party which makes extradition conditional on the existence of a treaty receives a request for extradition from another State Party with which it has no extradition treaty, it may consider this Convention as the legal basis for extradition in respect of such offences. Extradition shall be subject to the other conditions provided by the law of the requested State.
3. States Parties which do not make extradition conditional on the existence of a treaty shall recognize such offences as extraditable offences between themselves subject to the conditions provided by the law of the requested State.
4. Such offences shall be treated, for the purpose of extradition between States Parties, as if they had been committed not only in the place in which they occurred but also in the territories of the States required to establish their jurisdiction in accordance with article 5, paragraph!.

Article 9

1. States Parties shall afford one another the greatest measure of assistance in connection with criminal proceedings brought in respect of any of the offences referred to in article 4, including the supply of all evidence at their disposal necessary for the proceedings.
2. States Parties shall carry out their obligations under paragraph 1 of this article in conformity with any treaties on mutual judicial assistance that may exist between them.

Article 10

1. Each State Party shall ensure that, education and information regarding the prohibition against torture are fully included in the training of law enforcement personnel, civil or military, medical personnel, public officials and other persons who may be involved in the custody, interrogation or treatment of any individual subjected to any form of arrest, detention or imprisonment.
2. Each State Party shall include this prohibition in the rules or instructions issued in regard to the duties and functions of any such persons.

Article 11

Each State Party shall keep under systematic review interrogation rules, instructions, methods and practices as well as arrangements for the custody and treatment of persons subjected to any form of arrest, detention or imprisonment in any territory under its jurisdiction, with a view to preventing any cases of torture.

Article 12

Each State Party shall ensure that its competent authorities proceed to a prompt and impartial investigation, wherever there is reasonable ground to believe that an act of torture has been committed in any territory under its jurisdiction.

Article 13

Each State Party shall ensure that any individual who alleges he has been subjected to torture in any territory under its jurisdiction has the right to complain to, and to have his case promptly and impartially examined by, its competent authorities. Steps shall be taken to ensure that the complainant and witnesses are protected against all ill-treatment or intimidation as a consequence of his complaint or any evidence given.

Article 14

1. Each State Party shall ensure in its legal system that the victim of an act of torture obtains redress and has an enforceable right to fair and adequate compensation, including the means for as full rehabilitation as possible. In the event of the death of the victim as a result of an act of torture, his dependants shall be entitled to compensation.
2. Nothing in this article shall affect any right of the victim or other persons to compensation which may exist under national law.

Article 15

Each State Party shall ensure that any statement which is established to have been made as a result of torture shall not be invoked as evidence in any proceedings, except against a person accused of torture as evidence that the statement was made.

Article 16

1. Each State Party shall undertake to prevent in any territory under its jurisdiction other acts of cruel, inhuman or degrading treatment or punishment which do not amount to torture as defined in article 1, when such acts are committed by or at the instigation of or with the consent or acquiescence of a public official or other person acting in an official capacity- In particular, the obligations contained in articles 10, 11, 12 and 13 shall apply with the substitution for references to torture of references to other forms of cruel, inhuman or degrading treatment or punishment.

2. The provisions of this Convention are without prejudice to the provisions of any other international instrument or national law which prohibits cruel, inhuman or degrading treatment or punishment or which relates to extradition or expulsion.

PART II

Article 17

1. There shall be established a Committee against Torture (hereinafter referred to as the Committee) which shall carry out the functions hereinafter provided. The Committee shall consist often experts of high moral standing and recognized competence in the field of human rights, who shall serve in their personal capacity. The experts shall be elected by the States Parties, consideration being given to equitable geographical distribution and to the usefulness of the participation of some persons having legal experience.
2. The members of the Committee shall be elected by secret ballot from a list of persons nominated by States Parties. Each State Party may nominate one person from among its own nationals. States Parties shall bear in mind the usefulness of nominating persons who are also members of the Human Rights Committee established under the International Covenant on Civil and Political Rights and who are willing to serve on the Committee against Torture.
3. Elections of the members of the Committee shall be held at biennial meetings of States Parties convened by the Secretary-General of the United Nations. At those meetings, for which two thirds of the States Parties shall constitute a quorum, the persons elected

to the Committee shall be those who obtain the largest number of votes and an absolute majority of the votes of the representatives of States Parties present and voting.

4. The initial election shall be held no later than six months after the date of the entry into force of this Convention. At least four months before the date of each election, the Secretary-General of the United Nations shall address a letter to the States Parties inviting them to submit their nominations within three months. The Secretary-General shall prepare a list in alphabetical order of all persons thus nominated, indicating the States Parties which have nominated them, and shall submit it to the States Parties.
5. The members of the Committee shall be elected for a term of four years. They shall be eligible for re-election if renominated. However, the term of five of the members elected at the first election shall expire at the end of two years; immediately after the first election the names these five members shall be chosen by lot by the chairman of the meeting referred to in paragraph 3 of this article.
6. If a member of the Committee dies or resigns or for any other cause can no longer perform his Committee duties, the State Party which nominated him shall appoint another expert from among its nationals to serve for the remainder of his term, subject to the approval of the majority of the States Parties, The approval shall be considered given unless half or more of the States Parties respond negatively within six weeks after having been informed by the Secretary-General of the United Nations of the proposed appointment.

7. States Parties shall be responsible for the expenses of the members of the Committee while they are in performance of Committee duties.

Article 18

1. The Committee shall elect its officers for a term of two years. They may be re-elected.
2. The Committee shall establish its own rules of procedure, but these rules shall provide, inter alia, that:
   (a) Six members shall constitute a quorum;
   (b) Decisions of the Committee shall be made by a majority vote of the members present.
3. The Secretary-General of the United Nations shall provide the necessary staff and facilities for the effective performance of the functions of the Committee under this Convention.
4. The Secretary-General of the United Nations shall convene the initial meeting of the Committee. After its initial meeting, the Committee shall meet at such times as shall be provided in its rules of procedure.
5. The States Parties shall be responsible for expenses incurred in connection with the holding of meetings of the States Parties and of the Committee, including reimbursement to the United Nations for any expenses, such as the cost of staff and facilities, incurred by the United Nations pursuant to paragraph 3 of this article.

Article 19

1. The States Parties shall submit to the Committee, through the Secretary-General of the United Nations, reports on the measures they have taken to give

effect to their undertakings under this Convention, within one year after the entry into force of the Convention for the State Party concerned. Thereafter the States Parties shall submit supplementary reports every four years on any new measures taken and such other reports as the Committee may request.

2. The Secretary-General of the United Nations shall transmit the reports to all States Parties.
3. Each report shall be considered by the Committee which may make such general comments on the report as it may consider appropriate and shall forward these to the State Party concerned. That State Party may respond with any observations it chooses to the Committee.
4. The Committee may, at its discretion, decide to include any comments made by it in accordance with paragraph 3 of this article, together with the observations thereon received from the State Party concerned, in its annual report made in accordance with article 24. If so requested by the State Party concerned, the Committee may also include a copy of the report submitted under paragraph 1 of this article.

Article 20

1. If the Committee receives reliable information which appears to it to contain well-founded indications that, torture is being systematically practised in the territory of a State Party, the Committee shall invite that State Party to co-operate in the examination of the information and to this end to submit observations with regard to the information concerned.
2. Taking into account any observations which may

have been submitted by the State Party concerned, as well as any other relevant information available to it, the Committee may, if it decides that this is warranted, designate one or more of its members to make a confidential inquiry and to report to the Committee urgently.

3. If an inquiry is made in accordance with paragraph 2 of this article, the Committee shall seek the co-operation of the State Party concerned in agreement with that State Party, such an inquiry may include a visit to its territory.
4. After examining the findings of its member or members submitted in accordance with paragraph 2 of this article, the Committee shall transmit these findings to the State Party concerned together with any comments or suggestions which seem appropriate in view of the situation.
5. All the proceedings of the Committee referred to in paragraphs 1 to 4 of this article shall be confidential, and at all stages of the proceedings the co-operation of the State Party shall be sought. After such proceedings have been completed with regard to an inquiry made in accordance with paragraph 2, the Committee may, after consultations with the State Party concerned, decide to include a summary account of the results of the proceedings in its annual report made in accordance with article 24.

Article 21

1. A State Party to this Convention may at any time declare under this article that it recognizes the competence of the Committee to receive and consider communications to the effect that a State Party claims

that another State Party is not fulfilling its obligations under this Convention. Such communications may be received and considered according to the procedures laid down in this article only if submitted by a State Party which has made a declaration recognizing in regard to itself the competence of the Committee, No communication shall be dealt with by the Committee under this article if it concerns a State Party which has not made such a declaration. Communications received under this article shall be dealt with in accordance with the following procedure:

(a) If a State Party considers that another State Party is not giving effect to the provisions of this Convention, it may, by written communication, bring the matter to the attention of that State Party. Within three months after the receipt of the communication the receiving State shall afford the State which sent the communication an explanation or any other statement in writing clarifying the matter, which should include, to the extent possible and pertinent, reference to domestic procedures and remedies taken, pending or available in the matter;

(b) If the matter is not adjusted to the satisfaction of both States Parties concerned within six months after the receipt by the receiving State of the initial communication, either State shall have the right to refer the matter to the Committee, by notice given to the Committee and to the other State;

(c) The Committee shall deal with a matter referred to it under this article only after it has ascertained that all domestic remedies have been invoked and exhausted in the matter, in conformity with the generally recorded principles of international law. This shall not be we rule where the application of the remedies is unreasonably prolonged or is unlikely to bring effective relief to the person who is the victim of the violation of this Convention;

(d) The Committee shall hold closed meetings when examining communications under this article;

(e) Subject to the provisions of sub-paragraph (c), the Committee shall make available its good offices to the States Parties concerned with a view to a friendly solution of the matter on the basis of respect for the obligations provided for in this Convention. For this purpose, the Committee may, when appropriate, set up an *ad hoc* conciliation commission;

(f) In any matter referred to it under this article, the Committee may call upon the States Parties concerned, referred to in sub-paragraph *(b)*, to supply any relevant information;

(g) The States Parties concerned, referred to in sub-paragraph *(b)*, shall have the right to be represented when the matter is being considered by the Committee and to make submissions orally and/or in writing;

(h) The Committee shall, within twelve months after the date of receipt of notice under sub-paragraph *(b)*, submit a report:

(i) If a solution within the terms of sub-paragraph (e) is reached, the Committee shall confine its report to a brief statement of the facts and of the solution reached;

(ii) If a solution within the terms of sub-paragraph (e) is not reached, the Committee shall confine its report to a brief statement of the facts; the written submissions and record of the oral submissions made by the States Parties concerned shall be attached to the report.

In every matter, the report shall be communicated to the States Parties concerned.

2. The provisions of this article shall come into force when five States Parties to this Convention have made declarations under paragraph I of this article. Such declarations shall be deposited by the States Parties with the Secretary-General of the United Nations, who shall transmit copies thereof to the other States Parties. A declaration may be withdrawn at any time by notification to the Secretary-General. Such a withdrawal shall not prejudice the consideration of any matter which is the subject of a communication already transmitted under this article; no further communication by any State Party shall be received under this article after the notification of withdrawal of the declaration has been received by the Secretary-General, unless the State Party concerned has made a new declaration.

Article 22

1. A State Party to this Convention may at any time declare under this article that it recognizes the competence of the Committee to receive and consider communications from or on behalf of individuals

subject to its jurisdiction who claim to be victims of a violation by a State Party of the provisions of the Convention. No communication shall be received by the Committee if it concerns a State Party which has not made such a declaration.

2. The Committee shall consider inadmissible any communication under this article which is anonymous or which it considers to be an abuse of the right of submission of such communications or to be incompatible with the provisions of this Convention.
3. Subject to the provisions of paragraph 2, the Committee shall bring any communications submitted to it under this article to the attention of the State Party to this Convention which has made a declaration under paragraph 1 and is alleged to be violating any provisions of the Convention. Within six months, the receiving State shall submit to the Committee written explanations or statements clarifying the matter and the remedy, if any, that may have been taken by that State.
4. The Committee shall consider communications received under this article in the light of all information made available to it by or on behalf of the individual and by the State Party concerned.
5. The Committee shall not consider any communications from an individual under this article unless it has ascertained that:
   (a) The same matter has not been, and is not being, examined under another procedure of international investigation or settlement;
   (b) The individual has exhausted all available domestic remedies; this shall not be the rule

where the application of the remedies is unreasonably prolonged or is unlikely to bring effective relief to the person who is the victim of the violation of this Convention.

6. The Committee shall hold closed meetings when, examining communications under this article.
7. The Committee shall forward its views to the State Party concerned and to the individual.
8. The provisions of this article shall come into force when five States Parties to this Convention have made declarations under paragraph 1 of this article. Such declarations shall be deposited by the States Parties with the Secretary-General of the United Nations, who shall transmit copies thereof to the other States Parties. A declaration may be withdrawn at any time by notification to the Secretary-General. Such a withdrawal shall not prejudice the consideration of any matter which is the subject of a communication already transmitted under this article; no further communication by or on behalf of an individual shall be received under this article after the notification of withdrawal of the declaration has been received by the Secretary-General, unless the State Party has made a new declaration.

Article 23

The members of the Committee and of the ad hoc conciliation commissions which may be appointed under article 21, paragraph 1 (e), shall be entitled to the facilities, privileges and immunities of experts on mission for the United Nations as laid down in the relevant sections of the Convention on the Privileges and Immunities of the United Nations.

Article 24

The Committee shall submit an annual report on its activities under this Convention to the States Parties and to the General Assembly of the United Nations.

PART III

Article 25

1. This Convention is open for signature by all States.
2. This Convention is subject to ratification. Instruments of ratification shall be deposited with the Secretary-General of the United Nations.

Article 26

This Convention is open to accession by all States. Accession shall be effected by the deposit of an instrument of accession with the Secretary-General of the United Nations.

Article 27

1. This Convention shall enter into force on the thirtieth day after the date of the deposit with the Secretary-General of-the United Nations of the twentieth instrument of ratification or accession.
2. For each State ratifying this Convention or acceding to it after the deposit of the twentieth instrument of ratification or accession, the Convention shall enter into force on the thirtieth day after the date of the deposit of its own instrument of ratification or accession.

Article 28

1. Each State may, at the time of signature or ratification of this Convention or accession thereto, declare that it does not recognize the competence of the Committee provided for in article 20.

2. Any State Party having made a reservation in accordance with paragraph I of this article may, at any time, withdraw this reservation by notification to the Secretary-General of the United Nations.

Article 29

1. Any State Party to this Convention may propose an amendment and file it with the Secretary-General of the United Nations. The Secretary-General shall thereupon communicate the proposed amendment to the States Parties with a request that they notify him whether they favour a conference of States Parties for the purpose of considering and voting upon the proposal. In the event that within four months from the date of such communication at least one third of the States Parties favours such a conference, the Secretary-General shall convene the conference under the auspices of the United Nations. Any amendment adopted by a majority of the States Parties present and voting at the conference shall be submitted *by* the Secretary-General to all the States Parties for acceptance.
2. An amendment adopted in accordance with paragraph I of this article shall enter into force when two thirds of the States Parties to this Convention have notified the Secretary-General of the United Nations that they have accepted it in accordance with their respective constitutional processes.
3. When amendments enter into force, they shall be binding on those States Parties which have accepted them, other States Parties still being bound by the provisions of this Convention and any earlier amendments which they have accepted.

Article 30

1. Any dispute between two or more States Parties concerning the interpretation or application of this Convention which cannot be settled through negotiation shall, at the request of one of them, be submitted to arbitration. If within six months from the date of the request for arbitration the Parties are unable to agree on the organization of the arbitration, any one of those Parties may refer the dispute to the International Court of justice by request in conformity with the Statute of the Court.
2. Each State may, at the time of signature or ratification of this Convention or accession thereto, declare that it does not consider itself bound by paragraph I of this article. The other States Parties shall not be bound by paragraph I of this article with respect to any State Party having made such a reservation.
3. Any State Party having made a reservation in accordance with paragraph 2 of this article may at any time withdraw this reservation by notification to the Secretary-General of the United Nations.

Article 31

1. A State Party may denounce this Convention by written notification to the Secretary-General of the United Nations. Denunciation becomes effective one year after the date of receipt of the notification by the Secretary-General.
2. Such a denunciation shall not have the effect of releasing the State Party from its obligations under this Convention in regard to any act or omission which occurs prior to the date at which the denunciation becomes effective nor shall denunciation

prejudice in any way the continued consideration of any matter which is already under consideration by the Committee prior to the date at which the denunciation becomes effective.

3. Following the date at which the denunciation of a State Party becomes effective, the Committee shall not commence consideration of any new matter regarding that State.

Article 32

The Secretary-General of the United Nations shall inform all States Members of the United Nations and ail States which have signed this Convention or acceded to it of the following:

(a) Signatures, ratifications and accessions under articles 25 and 26;

(b) The date of entry into force of this Convention under article 27 and the date of the entry into force of any amendments under article 29;

(c) Denunciations under article 31.

Article 33

1. This Convention, of which the Arabic, Chinese, English, French, Russian and Spanish texts are equally authentic, shall be deposited with the Secretary-General of the United Nations.

2. The Secretary-General of the United Nations shall transmit certified copies of this Convention to all States.

APPENDIX–II

DECLARATION ON THE PROTECTION OF ALL PERSONS FROM BEING SUBJECTED TO TORTURE AND OTHER CRUEL, INHUMAN OR DEGRADING TREATMENT OR PUNISHMENT

Article 1

1. For the purpose of this Declaration, torture means any act by which severe pain or suffering, whether physical or mental, is intentionally inflicted by or at the instigation of a public official on a person for such purposes as obtaining from him or a third person information or confession, punishing him for an act he has committed or is suspected of having committed, or intimidating him or other persons. It does not include pain or suffering arising only from, inherent in or incidental to, lawful sanctions to the extent consistent with the Standard Minimum Rules for the Treatment of Prisoners.
2. Torture constitutes an aggravated and deliberate form of cruel, inhuman or degrading treatment or punishment.

Article 2

Any act of torture or other cruel, inhuman or degrading treatment or punishment is an offence to human dignity and shall be condemned as a denial of the purposes of the Charter of the United Nations and as a violation of the human rights and fundamental freedoms proclaimed in the Universal Declaration of Human Rights.

Article 3

No State may permit or tolerate torture or other cruel, inhuman or degrading treatment or punishment. Exceptional circumstances such as a state of war or a threat of war, internal political instability or any other public emergency may not be invoked as a justification of torture or other cruel, inhuman or degrading treatment or punishment.

Article 4

Each State shall, in accordance with the provisions of this Declaration, take effective measures to prevent torture and other cruel, inhuman or degrading treatment or punishment from being practised within its jurisdiction.

Article 5

The training of law enforcement personnel and of other public officials who may be responsible for persons deprived of their liberty shall ensure that full account is taken of the prohibition against torture and other cruel, inhuman or degrading treatment or punishment. This prohibition shall also, where appropriate, be included in such general rules or instructions as are issued in regard to the duties and functions of anyone who may be involved in the custody or treatment of such persons.

Article 6

Each State shall keep under systematic review interrogation methods and practices as well as arrangements for the custody and treatment of persons deprived of their liberty in its territory, with a view to preventing any cases of torture or other cruel, inhuman or degrading treatment or punishment.

Article 7

Each State shall ensure that all acts of torture as defined in article I are offences under its criminal law. The same shall apply in regard to acts which constitute participation in, complicity in, incitement to or an attempt to commit torture.

Article 8

Any person who alleges that he has been subjected to torture or other cruel, inhuman or degrading treatment or punishment by or at the instigation of a public official shall have the right to complain to, and to have his case impartially examined by, the competent authorities of the State concerned.

Article 9

Wherever there is reasonable ground to believe that an act of torture as defined in article 1 has been committed, the competent authorities of the State concerned shall promptly proceed to an impartial investigation even if there has been no formal complaint.

Article 10

If an investigation under article 8 or article 9 establishes that an act of torture as defined in article I appears to have been committed, criminal proceedings shall be instituted against the alleged offender or offenders in accordance with national law. If an allegation of other forms of cruel, inhuman or degrading treatment or punishment is considered to be well founded, the alleged offender or offenders shall be subject to criminal, disciplinary or other appropriate proceedings.

Article 11

Where it is proved that an act of torture or other cruel, inhuman or degrading treatment or punishment has been committed by or at the instigation of a public official, the victim shall be afforded redress and compensation in accordance with national law.

Article 12

Any statement which is established to have been made as a result of torture or other cruel, inhuman or degrading treatment or punishment may not be invoked as evidence against the person concerned or against any other person in any proceedings.

The Special Unrapporteur on Torture

Coinciding with the May 1998 sessions of the Committee against Torture (CAT) and the Board of Trustees of the Voluntary Fund for Victims of Torture, a meeting was held between the members of these two bodies, the Special Rapporteur on torture of the Commission on Human Rights and the High Commissioner. The Special Rapporteur has in the past met regularly with each of these bodies for information and coordination purposes.

However, this was the first meeting of the four United Nations mechanisms competent to deal with torture issues: a Joint Declaration was is sued in the context of the United Nations Inter national Day in Support of Victims of Torture (26 June 1998), an initiative which shows that efforts are being made to coordinate, support each other's activities and avoid duplication. It is important to note, however, that the nature of their respective mandates is very different and leaves little room for overlap ping.

Two of these mechanisms, the CAT and the Special Rapporteur, have a monitoring function. However, if the CAT, as a treaty-based body, is the primary mechanism in this respect, it is logical to ask for elucidation of the role of the Special Rapporteur and how they coordinate their activities. This is the issue we will try to clarify briefly in the following paragraphs. In addition, the Special Rapporteur is one of the extra-conventional mechanisms of the Commission with which he also establishes some kind of coordination. Mention will also be made in the present article of some aspects of that coordination.

In his report to the 1993 session of the Commission, the Special Rapporteur states that his mandate reflects the fact that the international community has come to the conclusion that the prohibition of torture is an obligation for all States, whether or not they have ratified a treaty which explicitly defines that prohibition. With regard to those States which have not ratified the two conventions incorporating the prohibition of torture (the International Covenant on Civil and Political Rights and the Convention against Torture), the Special Rapporteur is the only available mechanism. More important, however, than the difference in geographical scope is the difference in character between the mandates of the CAT and the Special Rapporteur which establishes their complementarity.

The essential task of the CAT is to determine whether a State party is complying with the provisions of the Convention. It does so through three different mechanisms set forth in the Convention: examination of the State's periodic reports, the individual complaints procedure - for those States that have explicitly accepted its competence in this respect - and the inquiry procedure in cases of systematic practice of torture, whenever its competence to do so is not explicitly excluded. *As* for the Special Rapporteur, his mandate deals mainly with allegations of torture in any part of the world. If both have the same ultimate objective (entering into dialogue with Governments to persuade them not to allow the occurrence of torture in situations falling under their respective jurisdictions), their methods differ: the CAT examines the way in which the Convention is implemented, the emphasis being on the legal and institutional framework of the State concerned; the Special Rapporteur seeks to clarify the veracity of allegations and to encourage Governments to provide remedies for the victims.

As specified in his methods of work', the Special Rapporteur carries out three main types of activities. None of them, with the exceptions indicated below, are common to the CAT and all are conducted in a way that minimizes the risk of interfering with the CAT's activities.

The first type of activity is the transmission of urgent appeals to Governments with a view to clarifying the situation of individuals Whose Circumstances give grounds for fearing that they are being or might be subjected to torture, ill-treatment. Urgent appeals, when appropriate, are transmitted jointly with other bodies of the UN human rights machinery, more specifically, the thematic and country extra-conventional mechanisms set up by the Commission on Human Rights. When dealing with general issues of particular importance the transmission of the appeal can be made public through a press release. The second type of activity is the transmission of allegations of individual cases as well as practices of torture based on credible and reliable reports received from inter-governrnental and non-governmental organizations as well as Governments.

The Special Rapporteur has developed a mechanism to follow-up the actions he undertakes. Thus, he analyses responses from Governments and transmits the contents to the sources of the allegations for comment. If these comments contain new information that complements or contradicts the Governments' responses, the allegations are again transmitted with the request that the Governments make new comments. In theory, this dialogue could be pursued, its aim being to exert influence on the Governments concerned with the objective of helping the alleged victim obtain redress. In practice, the dialogue on individual cases or on factors that facilitate the occurrence of torture in a country faces certain imponderables. Firstly, because more often than not

Governments do not respond to the allegations, even after receiving reminders, or reply simply by denying the facts. Secondly, because the sources of the information are not always in a position to pursue the cases and to keep the Special Rapporteur informed of developments, if any. On the other hand, the purpose of the exercise is not to adopt opinions on individual cases, like the Working Group on Arbitrary Detention, or to clarify cases, like the Working Group on Enforced or Involuntary Disappearances. The nature of a torture case is such that, in the absence of an independent judicial inquiry at the national level (a situation that occurs in the overwhelming majority of cases dealt with by the Special Rapporteur) it is almost impossible for the Special Rapporteur to ascertain that torture was inflicted in a particular case.

At the same time, the manner in which the individual cases are dealt with by the Special Rapporteur on the one hand, and by the CAT under the individual complaints procedure of the Convention on the other, is totally different, the latter being a quasi-judicial procedure that may conclude with the adoption of the Committee's views. In these circumstances, nothing prevents both mechanisms from dealing simultaneously or consecutively with the same case.

In recent years the Special Rapporteur has included observations on individual countries in his annual reports. This incipient practice allows him, *inter alia,* to comment on the information at his disposal and to refer to the concluding observations made by the CAT following examination of States' periodic reports. As for the CAT, its members constantly consult and make reference to the annual reports of the Special Rapporteur.

The third type of activity carried out by the Special Rapporteur concerns visits in *situ*. As indicated in *his* methods of work, the Special Rapporteur visits Countries on invitation, but also takes the initiative of approaching Governments when the information received suggests the existence of a significant incidence of torture. The country visits constitute a very important component of the mandate and non-governmental organisations often lobby the Special Rapporteur for a visit to the countries in which they are interested. Obtaining an invitation, however, is often the result of a long process. Several years can elapse from the time the request is first made until dates are agreed upon with the Government in question.

The visits allow the Special Rapporteur to enter into a constructive dialogue with all sectors concerned and to address recommendations to Governments. It is, undoubtedly, a much more effective mechanism than the simple exchange of correspondence. The recommendations attempt to be as precise as possible, since they are intended to yield concrete results. As a mechanism of follow-up, the Special Rapporteur periodically reminds Governments concerned of the observations and recommendations formulated and requests information on the consideration given to them as well as the steps taken for their implementation, or the constraints which might have prevented their implementation. In theory, the Special Rapporteur can make follow-up visits but in view of the universality of his mandate his priority is to visit as many countries as possible ill different regional groups. Follow-up visits have thus not been sought.

If the visit in itself can, and often does, have an impact on the Country concerned, long-term results should be pursued. Further mechanism should accordingly be developed to facilitate the implementation of the recommendations, the level of which remains low. It could be envisaged for example, that those recommendations are systematically taken into consideration when contemplating the possibility and defining the characteristics of a technical cooperation programme launched by the Office of the High Commissioner with respect to the country in question. This, obviously, also applies to the recommendations made by all the conventional and extra-conventional protection mechanisms.

As indicated earlier, the Special Rapporteur tries not only to coordinate his activities with the bodies competent on torture issues but also with the extra-conventional mechanisms of the Commission on Human Rights. This coordination has resulted in a few joint activities, the most salient being the frequent transmission of joint urgent appeals. Joint country visits have also taken place but were very limited in number. Among the thematic extra-conventional mechanisms, those which seem closer to the Special Rapporteur on torture are the Working Group on arbitrary detention, the Working Group on Enforced or Involuntary Disappearances and the Special Rapporteur on extrajudicial, summary or arbitrary executions. All deal with some of the most serious human rights violations, namely violations of the right to life, liberty and security as well as the right not to be subjected to torture or to cruel, inhuman or degrading treatment or punishment. In a given situation a clear relationship between violations of these rights often exists as they all have similar root causes. These causes may exhibit common features from one country to another but they also have specificities that have to be analysed with due regard to the national context in which they evolve.

A considerable amount of time and effort are spent by each of the above-mentioned mechanisms in assessing the circumstances in which the violations take place, their extent and possible remedies. These efforts are particularly exhaustive when they conduct country visits and elaborate the

Corresponding reports which are intended to be not only informative, but also to address specific recommendations to Governments. Moreover, each country visit should be given appropriate follow-up by the mechanism concerned with a view to pursuing the dialogue at the governmental and non-governmental levels and monitoring closely the implementation of the recommendations, an arduous task in itself. Coordination with human rights field operations is also an area that needs to be further explored, since the efforts made until now have yielded no concrete results. Under the present system, a country-oriented action for the protection of the above-mentioned basic human rights does not exist, with the obvious exceptions of the limited number of countries for which specific mandates have been established. And yet, that kind of action seems necessary if the efficiency of the thematic mechanisms and, ultimately, the whole system of protection are to be streamlined.

With that objective in mind, it would not be unreasonable to envisage a more integrated approach, taking the form of a single mechanism with an extended mandate that would replace at least the four mentioned above; a 'mechanism that, at the same time, would rationalize the scarce resources available. The pros and cons would, obviously, have to be carefully examined but it should be recognized that the present system is far from ideal, despite the efforts made by the experts and rapporteurs *to, inter alia,* coordinate their activities.

Joint Declaration of the Committee against Torture, the Board of Trustees of the Voluntary Fund for the Victims of Torture, the Special Rapporteur of the Commission on Human Rights on Questions relating to Torture and the High Commissioner for Human Rights

The Committee against Torture, the Board of Trustees of the Voluntary Fund for the Victims of Torture, the Special Rapporteur of the Commission on Human Rights on the questions relating to torture and the High Commissioner for Human Rights meeting at the United Nations Office at Geneva on 19 May 1998,

Recalling the appeal against torture of the High Commissioner for Human Rights, in Copenhagen, on 28 June 1994, in which he stated that ending torture is a beginning of true respect for the most basic of all human rights: the intrinsic dignity and value of each individual; *Welcoming* the decision of the General Assembly to declare 26 June the United Nations International Day in Support of Torture Victims; *Recognizing* that torture is one of the vilest acts to be perpetrated by human beings upon each other;

Recognizing that torture is prohibited by article 5 of the Universal Declaration of Human Rights;

Recognizing that torture is a breach of a nonderogable human right and a crime under international law;

Urge all States to ratify the United Nations Convention against Torture and Other Cruel, Inhuman or Degrading Treatment of Punishment without reservation, if they have not already done so;

Urge States Parties to the Convention which have not yet accepted its optional provisions to do so as soon as possible;

Urge all States to ensure that torture is a crime in their domestic law and to rigorously pursue perpetrators whenever the act was committed and bring them to justice;

Urge all States to provide compensation and rehabilitation for the victims of torture in their domestic law;

Urge all States to contribute to the United Nations Voluntary Fund for the Victims of Torture as fully and as often as they can;

Urge all States to cooperate with the United Nations Special Rapporteur on Torture in fulfilling its mandate when requested to do so;

Consider that, by these means the vile crime of torture maybe condemned and suppressed by all the people of the world.

It is obvious from foregoing description that torture during pre-trial and arbitrary detention or under trials and prisoners by police and security personnel in different parts of the world, are everyday occurrences most of which remain unnoticed to the public at large. But now due to wider access of communication media these heirous crimes and atrocities are frequently reported and opposed and condemned by civil society at large.

For a healthy social order, it is the primary duty of the state to man their police and security agencies with trained and skilled personnel with human attitude. In name of upholding righeousness and healthy social order, maintaining national integrity and sovereignty state can not peptrate inhuman treatment to the public.

APPENDIX–III

POLICE EXCESSES - TORTURE

Year 1993-1994

- Atrocity in police custody: alleged amputation of male organ of Shri Jugtaram in police custody, Barmer, Rajasthan
- Beating of Shri Luies, Advocate by Sub Inspector of Police- Complaint by Shri M. Udaya Bhanu, Advocate, Madras

Year 1997-1998

- Police torture and death, Rajasthan
- Compliance with the Commission's recommendations in the case of torture of Shri A. Ram Singh, a Member of the Cuddalore Bar Association, Tamil Nadu

Year 1998-1999

- A college lecturer becomes a victim of police brutality, Kerala (CASE NO:166/11/98-99)

Year 1999-2000

- Torture by Kerala police which led to the death of Hussain (CASE NO:64/11/1999-2000)
- Torture by Tiruchi police resulting in death of Shri Mohan (CASE NO:4444/95-96/NHRC)
- Custodial torture of Rakesh Kumar Vij,U.P. (CASE NO:12982/96-97)
- Death of an injured person owing to negligence by the police, Bihar (CASE NO:2054/4/1999-2000)Year

Year 2000-2001

- Fracture sustained by Sheshrao Rayasing Rathod

following police mistreatment, Maharashtra (CASE NO:1299/13/98-99)

Year 2001-2002

- Torture of Dayashankar by Police, U.P. (CASE NO:791/ 24/2000-2001)

Year 2002-2003

- Custodial torture of Zamir Ahmed Khan: Uttar Pradesh (Case No. 14071/24/2001-2002)
- Police beating of Jagdish Kawale leading to prievous injuries: Maharashtra (Case No.1585/13/2001-2002)
- Police high-handedness against a Teacher in Kota: Rajasthan (Case No.1603/20/2001-2002)

Year 2003-2004

- Harassment and Torture of Jagannath Shaw by the RPF Staff: West Bengal (Case No.118/25/2002-2003)
- Complaint from Sarita Sahu, Resident of Ranchi: Jharkhand (Case No. 974/34/2001-2002)

Year 2004-2005

- Torture and gang rape by police officers in Tripura - Case No. 5/23/2003-2004-WC
- Suicide by Vinod Kumar Rajput due to police harassment-Case No.1412/12/98-99(FC)

ILLEGAL DETENTION

Year 1995-1996

- Commission investigates complaints of police high-handedness against the villagers of Mannikere, Karnataka

Year 1997-1998

- Illegal detention/ torture by the police- complaint from Shri Baba Khan, Rajasthan

- Compensation for illegal detention- complaint from Shri Ranbir Yadav, U.P.

Year 1999-2000

- Illegal detention/abduction of Rama Rao by Andhra Police (CASE NO:5828/95-96/NHRC)

Year 2001-2002

- Illegal detention and torture of Anil Kumar, Maharashtra (CASE NO:517/13/98-99)
- Illegal detention by Police, U.P. (CASE NO:13161/ 24/98-99)
- Illegal detention and torture of D.M. Rege, Maharashtra (CASE NO:1427/13/98-99)

Year 2002-2003

- Negligence of police personnel leading to wrongful confinement of lkram-ud-din: Uttar Pradesh (Case No.23239/24/1999-2000)

Year 2003-2004

- Unlawful Detention of Manoharan: Tamil Nadu (Case No.213/22/2001-2002)
- Illegal Detention and Torture in Police Station, Shikarpur: Uttar Pradesh (Case No.17171/24/1999-2000)

Year 2004-2005

- Illegal detention of two Adivasi boys by Kerala Police - Case No. 208/11/97-98
- Illegal detention of S/Sh. Ramveer Singh, Surendra Singh Delhi - Case No. 3454/30/2000-2001
- Illegal detention and torture of Shri Zamir Ahmed by the police at Sayana, Bulandshahr, UttarPradesh-Case No: 14071/24/2001-2002

FALSE IMPLICATION

Year 1999-2000

- False implication and torture of Sh. Rajiv Rattan by the police (CASE NO:9302/95-96)

Year 2000-2001

- False implication of the Complainant and others and Torture by Police, Delhi (CASE NO:3069/30/1999-2000)

Year 2001-2002

- False implication of Madhukar Jetley, U.P. (CASE NO:2385/24/2000-2001)
- False implication of Rajinder Singh, Haryana (CASE NO:810/7/98-99)
- False implication of Manoj Kumar Tak and Narender Tak ,Madhya Pradesh (CASE NO:667/12/98-99-FC)

Year 2002-2003

- False implication of navi Ullah under NDPS Act: Uttar Pradesh (Case No. 13501/24/2000-2001)

OTHER POLICE EXCESSES

Year 1997-1998

- Failure in taking action by police, J&K
- Compensation to the victims of highhandedness of PAC personnel at ASI Ghat, Varanasi, U.P.

Year 1998-1999

- Police harassment of Shri Shakuni Choudhary,MLA Bihar (CASE NO:641/95-96/NHRC)
- Policemen turn robbers and kill innocent citizens (CASE NO:144/93-94/NHRC)

Year 1999-2000

- High Handed acts of police, U.P. (CASE NO:1970/94-95/NHRC)

Year 2000-2001

- Harassment by police leads to suicide of Surinder Singh, U.P.(CASE NO:1929/96-97)
- Police High-handedness against agitating farmers in ten Villages of C.R. Pattna Taluk, Hassan Distt. Karnataka (CASE NO:91/10/1998-99)
- Acts of police High-Handedness against Dalits in Ogalure Village, Tamil Nadu (CASE NO:772/22/98-99)

Year 2003-2004

- Death of Salman Dinkar Padvi in Police Firing: Maharashtra (Case No.1332/13/2000-2001/FC)
- Death of Sonali Bose in a Shoot out by Police in Agra: Uttar Pradesh (Case No.13664/24/2002/2003-FC)

[Source: NHRC, India].

APPENDIX–IV

CHRONOLOGY OF EVENTS REGARDING HUMAN RIGHTS IN INDIA

- 1829 - The practice of sati was formally abolished by Governor General William Bentick after years of campaigning by Hindu reform movements such as the Brahmo Samaj of Ram Mohan Roy against this orthodox Hindu funeral custom of self-immolation of widows after the death of their husbands.
- 1929 - *Child Marriage Restraint Act*, prohibiting marriage of minors under 14 years of age is passed.
- 1947 - India achieves political independence from the British Raj.
- 1950 - The Constitution of India establishes a sovereign democratic republic with universal adult franchise. Part 3 of the Constitution contains a Bill of Fundamental Rights enforceable by the Supreme Court and the High Courts. It also provides for reservations for previously disadvantaged sections in education, employment and political representation.
- 1952 - Criminal Tribes Acts repealed by government, former "criminal tribes" categorized as "denotified" and Habitual Offenders Act (1952) enacted.
- 1955 - Reform of family law concerning Hindus gives more rights to Hindu women.
- 1958 -Armed Forces (Special Powers) Act, 1958-[3]
- 1973 - Supreme Court of India rules in *Kesavananda Bharati case* that the basic structure of the Constitution (including many fundamental rights) is unalterable by a constitutional amendment.

- 1975-77 - State of Emergency in India - extensive rights violations take place.
- 1978 - SC rules in *Maneka Gandhi v. Union of India* that the right to life under Article 21 of the Constitution cannot be suspended even in an emergency.
- 1978-Jammu and Kashmir Public Safety Act, 1978.
- 1984 - Operation Blue Star and the subsequent 1984 Anti-Sikh riots
- 1985-6 - The Shah Bano case, where the Supreme Court recognised the Muslim woman's right to maintenance upon divorce, sparks protests from Muslim clergy. To nullify the decision of the Supreme Court, the Rajiv Gandhi government enacted The Muslim Women (Protection of Rights on Divorce) Act 1986
- 1989 - *Scheduled Caste and Scheduled Tribe (Prevention of Atrocities) Act, 1989* is passed.
- 1989–present - Kashmiri insurgency sees ethnic cleansing of Kashmiri Pandits, desecrating Hindu temples, killing of Hindus and Sikhs, and abductions of foreign tourists and government functionaries.
- 1992 - A constitutional amendment establishes Local Self-Government (Panchayati Raj) as a third tier of governance at the village level, with one-third of the seats reserved for women. Reservations were provided for scheduled castes and tribes as well.
- 1992 - Babri Masjid demolished by Hindu mobs, resulting in riots across the country.
- 1993 - National Human Rights Commission is established under the *Protection of Human Rights Act.*

- 2001 - Supreme Court passes extensive orders to implement the right to food.
- 2002 - Violence in Gujarat, chiefly targeting its Muslim minority, claims many lives.
- 2005 - A powerful *Right to Information Act* is passed to give citizen's access to information held by public authorities.
- 2005 - *National Rural Employment Guarantee Act (NREGA)* guarantees universal right to employment.
- 2006 - Supreme Court orders police reforms in response to the poor human rights record of Indian police.
- 2009 - Delhi High Court delcares that Section 377 of the Indian Penal Code, which outlaws a range of unspecified "unnatural" sex acts, is unconstitutional when applied to homosexual acts between private consenting individuals, effectively decriminalising homosexual relationships in India.

Glossary

Affirmative Action: Action taken by a government or private institution to make up for past discrimination in education, work, or promotion on the basis of gender, race, ethnic origin, religion, or disability.

Civil and Political Rights: The rights of citizens to liberty and equality; sometimes referred to as first generation rights. Civil rights include freedom to worship, to think and express oneself, to vote, to take part in political life, and to have access to information.

Codification, Codify: The process of bringing customary international law to written form.

Collective Rights: The rights of groups to protect their interests and identities.

Commission on Human Rights: Body formed by the Economic and Social Council (ECOSOC) of the UN to deal with human rights; one of the first and most important international human rights bodies.

Convention: Binding agreement between states; used synonymously with Treaty and Covenant. Conventions are stronger than Declarations because they are legally binding for governments that have signed them. When the UN General Assembly adopts a convention, it creates international norms and standards. Once a convention is adopted by the UN General Assembly, Member States can then Ratify the convention, promising to uphold it. Governments that violate the standards set forth in a convention can then be censured by the UN.

Convention on the Elimination of all Forms of Discrimination Against Women (Women's Convention) (adopted 1979; entered into force 1981): The first legally binding international document prohibiting discrimination against women and obligating governments to take affirmative steps to advance the equality of women.

Convention on the Rights of the Child (Children's Convention) (adopted 1989; entered into force 1990): Convention setting forth a full spectrum of civil, cultural, economic, social, and political rights for children.

Covenant: Binding agreement between states; used synonymously with Convention and Treaty. The major international human rights covenants, both passed in 1966, are the International Covenant on Civil and Political Rights (ICCPR) and the International Covenant on Economic, Social and Cultural Rights (ICESCR).

Customary International Law: Law that becomes binding on states although it is not written, but rather adhered to out of custom; when enough states have begun to behave as though something is law, it becomes law "by use"; this is one of the main sources of international law.

Declaration: Document stating agreed upon standards but which is not legally binding. UN conferences, like the 1993 UN Conference on Human Rights in Vienna and the 1995 World Conference for Women in Beijing, usually produce two sets of declarations: one written by government representatives and one by Nongovernmental Organizations (NGOs). The UN General Assembly often issues influential but legally Nonbinding declarations.

Economic and Social Council (ECOSOC): A UN council of 54 members primarily concerned with population, economic development, human rights, and criminal justice. This high-ranking body receives and issues human rights reports in a variety of circumstances.

Economic, Social, Cultural Rights: Rights that concern the production, development, and management of material for the necessities of life. The right to preserve and develop one's cultural identity. Rights that give people social and economic security, sometimes referred to as security-oriented or second generation rights. Examples are the right to food, shelter, and health care.

Environmental, Cultural, and Developmental Rights: Sometimes referred to as third generation rights, these rights recognize that people have the right to live in a safe and healthy environment and that groups of people have the right to cultural, political, and economic development.

Genocide: The systematic killing of people because of their race or ethnicity.

Human Rights: The rights people are entitled to simply because they are human beings, irrespective of their citizenship, nationality, race, ethnicity, language, gender, sexuality, or abilities; human rights become enforceable when they are Codified as Conventions, Covenants, or Treaties, or as they become recognized as Customary International Law.

Human Rights Community: A community based on human rights, where respect for the fundamental dignity of each individual is recognized as essential to the functioning and advancement of society. A community that works to uphold each article of the UDHR.

Inalienable: Refers to rights that belong to every person and cannot be taken from a person under any circumstances.

Indigenous Peoples: People who are original or natural inhabitants of a country. Native Americans, for example, are the indigenous peoples of the United States.

Indivisible: Refers to the equal importance of each human rights law. A person cannot be denied a right because someone decides it is "less important" or "nonessential."

Interdependent: Refers to the complementary framework of human rights law. For example, your ability to participate in your government is directly affected by your right to express yourself, to get an education, and even to obtain the necessities of life.

Intergovernmental Organizations (IGOs): Organizations sponsored by several governments that seek to coordinate their efforts; some are regional (e.g., the Council of Europe, the Organization of African Unity), some are alliances (e.g., the North Atlantic Treaty Organization, NATO); and some are dedicated to a specific purpose (e.g., the UN Centre for Human Rights, and The United Nations Education, Scientific and Cultural Organization, UNESCO).

International Bill of Human Rights: The combination of the Universal Declaration of Human Rights (UDHR), the International Covenant on Civil and Political Rights (ICCPR) and its optional Protocol, and the International Covenant on Economic, Social, and Cultural Rights (ICESCR).

International Covenant on Civil and Political Rights (ICCPR): Adopted in 1966, and entered into force in 1976. The ICCPR declares that all people have a broad range of civil and political rights. One of the components of the International Bill of Human Rights.

International Covenant on Economic, Social, and Cultural

Rights (ICESCR): Adopted 1966, and entered into force 1976. The ICESCR declares that all people have a broad range of economic, social, and cultural rights. One of the components of the International Bill of Human Rights.

International Labor Organization (ILO): Established in 1919 as part of the Versailles Peace Treaty to improve working conditions and promote social justice; the ILO became a Specialized Agency of the UN in 1946.

Legal Rights: Rights that are laid down in law and can be defended and brought before courts of law.

Member States: Countries that are members of the United Nations.

Moral Rights: Rights that are based on general principles of fairness and justice; they are often but not always based on religious beliefs. People sometimes feel they have a moral right even when they do not have a legal right. For example, during the civil rights movement in the USA, protesters demonstrated against laws forbidding Blacks and Whites to attend the same schools on grounds that these laws violated their moral rights.

Natural Rights: Rights that belong to people simply because they are human beings.

Nonbinding: A document, like a Declaration, that carries no formal legal obligations. It may, however, carry moral obligations or attain the force of law as Customary International Law.

Nongovernmental Organizations (NGOs): Organizations formed by people outside of government. NGOs monitor the proceedings of human rights bodies such as the Commission on Human Rights and are the "watchdogs" of the human rights that fall within their mandate. Some are large and international (e.g., the Red Cross,

Amnesty International, the Girl Scouts); others may be small and local (e.g., an organization to advocate for people with disabilities in a particular city; a coalition to promote women's rights in one refugee camp). NGOs play a major role in influencing UN policy, and many of them have official consultative status at the UN.

Political Rights: The right of people to participate in the political life of their communities and society. For example, the right to vote for their government or run for office. See Civil and Political Rights.

Protocol: A treaty which modifies another treaty (e.g., adding additional procedures or substantive provisions).

Ratification, Ratify: Process by which the legislative body of a state confirms a government's action in signing a treaty; formal procedure by which a state becomes bound to a treaty after acceptance.

Reservation: The exceptions that States Parties make to a treaty (e.g., provisions that they do not agree to follow). Reservations, however, may not undermine the fundamental meaning of the treaty.

Self-Determination: Determination by the people of a territorial unit of their own political future without coercion from powers outside that region.

Signing, Sign: In human rights the first step in ratification of a treaty; to sign a Declaration, Convention, or one of the Covenants constitutes a promise to adhere to the principles in the document and to honor its spirit.

State: Often synonymous with "country"; a group of people permanently occupying a fixed territory having common laws and government and capable of conducting international affairs.

States Party(ies): Those countries that have Ratified a

Covenant or a Convention and are thereby bound to conform to its provisions.

Treaty: Formal agreement between states that defines and modifies their mutual duties and obligations; used synonymously with Convention and Covenant. When conventions are adopted by the UN General Assembly, they create legally binding international obligations for the Member States who have signed the treaty. When a national government Ratifies a treaty, the articles of that treaty become part of its domestic legal obligations.

United Nations Charter: Initial document of the UN setting forth its goals, functions, and responsibilities; adopted in San Francisco in 1945.

United Nations General Assembly: One of the principal organs of the UN, consisting representatives of all member states. The General Assembly issues Declarations and adopts Conventions on human rights issues, debates relevant issues, and censures states that violate human rights. The actions of the General Assembly are governed by the United Nations Charter.

Universal Declaration of Human Rights (UDHR): Adopted by the general assembly on December 10, 1948. Primary UN document establishing human rights standards and norms. All member states have agreed to uphold the UDHR. Although the declaration was intended to be Nonbinding, through time its various provisions have become so respected by States that it can now be said to be Customary International Law.

Bibliography

Arambulo, Kitty. *Strengthening the Supervision of the International Covenant on Economic, Social and Cultural Rights: Theoretical and Procedural Aspects*. Oxford, UK: Hart, 1999

Bartlett, Peter, ed. *Mental Disability and the European Convention on Human Rights*. Leiden: E.J. Brill, 2006.

Bauer, Joanne R. and Daniel A. Bell, eds. *The East Asian Challenge for Human Rights*. Cambridge, UK: Cambridge University Press, 1999.

Bayefsky, Anne F. *The UN Human Rights Treaty System: Universality at the Crossroads*. Ardsley, NY: Transnational Publ., 2001.

Boerefijn, Ineke. *The Reporting Procedure Under the Covenant on Civil and Political Rights: Practices and Procedure of the Human Rights Committee*. Oxford, UK: Hart, 1999.

Broomhall, Bruce. *International Justice & The International Criminal Court: Between Sovereignty and the Rule of Law*. New York: Oxford University Press, 2003.

Brownlie, Ian and Guy S. Goodwin-Gill, eds. *Basic Documents on Human Rights*. New York: Oxford University Press, 5th ed., 2006.

Campbell, Tom, Jeffrey Goldsworthy, and Adrienne Stone, eds. *Protecting Human Rights: Instruments and Institutions*. New York: Oxford University Press, 2003.

Cassese, Antonio. *Human Rights in a Changing World*. Cambridge, UK: Polity Press, 1990.

Chandler, David. *From Kosovo to Kabul and Beyond: Human Rights and International Intervention*. London: Pluto Press, 2006 ed.

Chandler, David, ed. *Rethinking Human Rights: Critical Approaches to International Politics*. New York: Palgrave Macmillan, 2002.

Chapman, Audrey and Sage Russell, eds. *Core Obligations: Building a Framework for Economic, Social and Cultural Rights*. New York, Transnational Publ., 2002.

Chatterjee, Deen K. and Don E. Scheid, eds. *Ethics and Foreign Intervention*. Cambridge, UK: Cambridge University Press, 2003.

Chesterman, Simon. *Just War or Just Peace? Humanitarian Intervention and International Law*. New York: Oxford University Press, 2001.

Clapham, Andrew. *Human Rights in the Private Sphere*. New York: Oxford University Press, 1994.

Clapham, Andrew. *Human Rights Obligations of Non-State Actors*. New York: Oxford University Press, 2006.

Claude, Richard Pierre and Burns H. Weston, eds. *Human Rights in the World Community: Issues and Action*. Philadelphia, PA: University of Pennsylvania Press, 1992.

Clayton, Richard and Hugh Tomlinson. *The Law of Human Rights*. New York: Oxford University Press, 2006.

Çoban, Ali Riza. *Protection of Property Rights within the European Convention on Human Rights*. Aldershot: Ashgate, 2004.

Conte, Alex, Scott Davidson, and Richard Burchill. *Defining Civil and Political Rights: The Jurisprudence of the United Nations Human Rights Committee*. Aldershot: Ashgate, 2004.

Cook, Rebecca J., ed. *Human Rights of Women: National and International Perspectives*. Philadelphia, PA: University of Pennsylvania Press, 1994.

Cook Rebecca J., Bernard M. Dickens and Mahmoud F. Fathalla. *Reproductive Health and Human Rights: Integrating Medicine, Ethics and Law*. New York: Oxford University Press, 2003.

Cottier, Thomas, Joost Pauwelyn, and Elisabeth Bürgi, eds. *Human Rights and International Trade*. New York: Oxford University Press, 2005.

Donnelly, Jack. *International Human Rights*. Boulder, CO: Westview Press, 2006.

Drzemczewski, Andrew Z. *European Human Rights Convention in Domestic Law: A Comparative Study*. New York: Oxford University Press, 1983.

Evans, Carolyn. *Freedom of Religion under the European Convention on Human Rights*. New York: Oxford University Press, 2001.

Evans, Tony. *The Politics of Human Rights: A Global Perspective*. London: Pluto Press, 2005.

Forsythe, David P. *Human Rights in International Relations*. Cambridge, UK: Cambridge University Press, 2000.

Fortin, Jane. *Children's Rights and the Developing Law*. Cambridge, UK: Cambridge University Press, 2003.

Franklin, Bob, ed. *The New Handbook of Children's Rights: Comparative Policy and Practice*. London: Routledge, 2002.

Gearty, Conor. *Principles of Human Rights Adjudication*. New York: Oxford University Press, 2004.

Gewirth, Alan. *Human Rights*. Chicago, IL: University of Chicago Press, 1982.

Hathaway, James C. *The Rights of Refugees under International Surface*. Cambridge, UK: Cambridge University Press, 2005.

Hayden, Patrick, ed. *The Philosophy of Human Rights*. St. Paul, MN: Paragon House, 2001.

Jokic, Aleksander, ed. *Humanitarian Intervention: Moral and Philosophical Issues*. Orchard Park, NY: Broadview Press, 2003.

Joseph, Sarah, Jenny Schultz, and Melissa Castan. *The International Covenant on Civil and Political Rights: Cases, Materials, and Commentary*. New York: Oxford University Press, 2004.

Keal, Paul. *European Conquest and the Rights of Indigenous Peoples: The Moral Backwardness of International Society*. Cambridge, UK: Cambridge University Press, 2003.

Kent, Ann E. *China, the United Nations, and Human Rights: The Limits of Compliance*. Philadelphia, PA: University of Pennsylvania Press, 1999.

Kent, George. *Freedom From Want: The Human Right to Adequate Food*. Washington, DC: Georgetown University Press, 2005.

Keown, Damien V., Charles S. Prebish, and Wayne R. Husted, eds. *Buddhism and Human Rights*. Richmond, England, 1998.

Kolodziej, Edward A., ed. *A Force Profonde: The Power, Promise, and Politics of Human Rights*. Philadelphia, PA: University of Pennsylvania Press, 2003.

Kumar, Arvind. *Encyclopaedia of Human Rights: Violence and Non-violence* (3 vols.), New Delhi, Anmol, 1998.

Kymlicka, Will, ed. *The Rights of Minority Cultures*. New York: Oxford University Press, 1995.

Landman, Todd. *Protecting Human Rights: A Comparative Study*. Washington, DC: Georgetown University Press, 2005.

Langlois, Anthony J. *The Politics of Justice and Human Rights: Southeast Asia and Universalist Theory*. Cambridge, UK: Cambridge University Press, 2001.

Lester, Lord and D. Oliver, eds. *Constitutional Law and Human Rights*. London: Butterworths, 1997.

Lijnzaad, Liesbeth. *Reservations to UN Human Rights Treaties: Ratify or Ruin?* Dordrecht: Nijhoff, 1995.

Mahoney, Jack. *The Challenge of Human Rights: Origin, Development, and Significance.* Malden, MA: Blackwell, 2007.

Nickel, James W. *Making Sense of Human Rights*. Malden, MA: Blackwell, 2nd ed., 2006.

Nino, Carlos Santiago. *The Ethics of Human Rights.* New York: Oxford University Press, 1991.

Shah, Giriraj & KN. Gupta, *Human Rights: Free and Equal,* New Delhi, Anmol, 2007.

Sigler, Jay A. *Minority Rights: A Comparative Analysis.* Westport, CT: Greenwood Press, 1983.

Singh, T. Hemo, *Manipur Imbroglio,* Newe Delhi: Akansha, 2009.

Sinha, P.C., *International Encyclopaedia of Human Rights and Law* (3 vols.), New Delhi, Anmol, 2006.

Steiner, Henry J. and Philip Alston. *International Human Rights in Context: Law, Politics, Morals.* New York: Oxford University Press, 2000.

Sullivan, Rory, ed. *Business and Human Rights: Dilemmas and Solutions*. Sheffield, UK: Greenleaf Publ., 2003.

Talbott, William J. *Which Rights Should Be Universal?* New York: Oxford University Press, 2005.

INDEX

■■■